GARLAND STUDIES ON

THE ELDERLY IN AMERICA

edited by
STUART BRUCHEY
UNIVERSITY OF MAINE

A GARLAND SERIES

HISPANIC ELDERS
AND HUMAN SERVICES

SARA ALEMÁN

GARLAND PUBLISHING, Inc.
NEW YORK & LONDON / 1997

Library of Congress Cataloging-in-Publication Data

Alemán, Sara, 1944–
    Hispanic elders and human services / Sara Alemán.
        p.   cm. — (Garland studies on the elderly in America)
    Originally presented as the author's thesis (Ph. D.—Brandeis
University, 1993).
    Includes bibliographical references and index.
    ISBN 0-8153-2548-7 (alk. paper)
    1. Hispanic American aged—Services for. 2. Hispanic
American aged—Social conditions. I. Title. II. Series.
HV1461.A5486 1997
362.6'3'08968073—dc21   96-39601

Printed on acid-free, 250-year-life paper
Manufactured in the United States of America

Dedication

Isidore Siebenberg
and
James Terry Alemán Burns

Contents

Tables

Preface

In my family children never talked about age but we were instructed and socialized on how to behave towards elders. In Mexican American families as well as in other Hispanic families, children learn at a very early age that one pays respect to elders whether that person is known or is a stranger. In practice, we learn to respect anyone who is older than oneself.

As I became aware of myself, I began to appreciate my parents as well as my brothers and sisters. Others say that this process is a sign of maturity and the beginning of one's own acquisition of wisdom. I believe this is true.

Having been raised in a very traditional Mexican family, I grew up being courteous, accommodating, and polite to elders. Interestingly, these behaviors and attitudes have translated themselves into a life-long feeling of respect and protectiveness towards all individuals but particularly elders. This may be because my parents told us stories that depicted pride (an inherited characteristic) and physical suffering (due to lack of resources) and humiliation (due to discrimination).

The issue of my personal identity was clarified at a very early age by my parents not by the larger society. When I was in grade school, I was given a questionnaire to complete. I took it home and asked my father, "Am I White or Black or Other?" He answered, "We're Caucasians and we're also Mexicans. Never forget who you are."

In this book, I use the terms Mexican American and Cuban Americans. These terms are used to describe individuals who may have been born in their native country or in the United States but who currently live in the United States. They are some of the participants in this study.

The term Hispanic is used because this is the term used by The Commonwealth Fund Commission in its data collection. The term Latino may have also been appropriately used due to its focus on a cultural identity of people rather than on a language. However, for the sake of being consistent with the funding agency's choice of terminology, I used the term Hispanic.

Books such as this are important because of the information they provide to the larger society and to service providers who need to be prepared to work with ethnic elders and avoid the mistakes of the past. Also, a person's culture can no longer be ignored if we intend to help people reach their potential. Culture serves as a guide (Henderson 1993) that helps service providers understand behaviors, values and interactions. Therefore, it is an integral component of all ethnic populations. It is in understanding and appreciating differences that service providers can move forward to the development of culturally appropriate services.

The Hispanic elder is of great interest to scholars and service providers because of demographics that project a dramatic increase in their numbers. For me, an additional interest is the desire to add to the knowledge base.

I thank *los viejitos*, Zulema and Eleuterio, for my own knowledge base. They gave me my culture, my love of the larger *familia* and love of my siblings. This knowledge has been the foundation of all subsequent learning.

I appreciate all my brothers and sisters for their love, encouragement and support. They are Louis, Marcos, Elizabeth, Ismael, Teofilo, Efraim, Josúe, María de la Paz, Ester and Eleazar.

Acknowledgments are also in order. My sincere appreciation to my dear friend and mentor, Dr. Fran Bernat who saw the value in this work and encouraged me to continue. VeeDochia Peart, Trisha McMahon, Scott Watkins, Rose Lejman and Mary Flores were always willing to help with the technical details of the book. I also want to thank The Commonwealth Fund Commission for funding this research. The current political climate has made it difficult for federal agencies to fund studies to explore diversity issues. Private funds from corporations that see the importance of learning about each other, such as The Commonwealth Fund Commission, enable us to continue this important research. The hope is that we learn about diverse populations and improve our understanding about each other.

Thank you also to my colleagues who have been so encouraging and left me alone while I worked: Jerry Finn, Vi McLean, Pat Spakes, Eufemia Amabisca and Paul Luken. Thanks also to Ken Jones, Carole

Upshur, Susan Lanspery, Miguel Montiel and Allan Brawley for their mentoring.

Hispanic Elders and
Human Services

I

Introduction

STATEMENT OF PURPOSE

This work argues that community-based services are used differently by elderly Mexican Americans, Puerto Ricans, and Cubans. The study looks at Hispanic elders, their characteristics, and policies and strategies that need to be explored and possibly implemented in an attempt to reach the many Hispanics who are similarly needy. The study will look at Hispanic elders who have gained access to the community-based system. Further focus will be on frail elders. For purposes of this study, frail Hispanic elders will be described as those who identified themselves as being impaired in their performance of two or more activities of daily living (ADLs) and at least one instrumental activity of daily living (IADL). The frail category also includes those elders who have two or more ADL limitations and no IADL limitations or four or more IADL limitations and no ADL limitations.

Demographic data and research reveal that elderly Hispanics, as a group, are growing in absolute numbers and as a proportion of the total of the United States population.[1] Currently, Hispanics 65 years of age and older comprise approximately three percent of the elderly population in the United States. Between 1970 and 1980, this population grew by 61 percent while the elderly population as a whole grew by just 40 percent.[2] By 2020, the elderly Hispanic population is expected to quadruple[3] to approximately four million people, increasing from three to eight percent of the total elderly population.[4]

NEED FOR THIS STUDY

This study is important for several reasons. The first is the need to examine ethnic differences and similarities. Previous studies have tended to treat all Hispanics as a single ethnic group, masking important ethnic-specific characteristics.[5] It is now important to consider ethnic differences and similarities for the subgroups within the Hispanic population. The subgroups differ in part because, among other things, they come from different countries with different cultural norms and values. However, much of the available literature does not differentiate one group from another. Grouping all Hispanics into one group has led to problems in applying research findings to specific subgroups.[6] Additionally, it is difficult to make policy recommendations regarding one subgroup when research was carried out with another subgroup. While there are similarities in such areas as language, food preferences, and attitudes toward government, there are more differences than are generally known.[7] These differences need to be considered when making policies and developing programs. A Mexican American elderly person may be as different from a Colombian elderly person as from a Polish elder due to intra-cultural variation.[8]

Another reason for this study is to address the special needs of Mexican American elders: the Mexican American subgroup of elderly is the fastest growing of the Hispanic elderly population. In spite of the growth in this population, few policy recommendations have addressed the future needs of these elders and their families. These Hispanic elders tend to have higher levels of need than do nonminority elders.[9] According to Juarez (1988),[10] during the period between 1980 and 2000 the population of Mexican elders over 60 years of age is expected to increase by 100 percent.

Gender differences within Mexican American elders is the third reason for studying these elders. Elderly Mexican American females will increase in even greater numbers and are more economically disadvantaged than their male counterparts.[11] Gender differences will be studied with this elderly population in an attempt to provide some knowledge about gender-specific distinctions that may be found in this population. Few studies have been able to identify whether different needs exist for elderly Mexican American females and elderly Mexican

American males. Any information on gender differences will contribute to the current body of available information.

The fourth reason is the need to learn more about educational levels and the ability to speak English. Some studies[12] have shown strong positive correlations between levels of education and ability to access needed services, i.e., transportation, medical care, etc. These same studies reflect a strong correlation between the ability of elders to communicate in English and their ability to access formal support services. In spite of this data, current available information still reflects that only 49.5 percent of Mexican Americans finish high school[13] and the national dropout rate for all Hispanics is 43 percent.[14] Given that Lubben and Becerra (1987)[15] found that only 16 percent of elderly Mexican Americans had completed high school, in three generations there has only been an increase of 33 percent in high school graduates. Additionally, it is alarming that 50.5 percent of current Mexican Americans are not finishing school.[16] This will place them at a high socioeconomic disadvantage in the future as they, too, age. Further, this disadvantage impacts on the elderly because, given limited educational levels and continued low incomes of the younger generation[17] how great of a resource can this group continue to be for their elders? Another question concerns what will happen as the undereducated young people of today age and themselves need services. In order to fully address the policy implications of future service utilization, both formal and informal, the educational issue needs attention. Any development of policies needs to consider both the current elderly who, through overt discrimination policies of the past, experienced limited opportunities and the younger Mexican Americans who, for still other undefined reasons, are not able to take advantage of the educational opportunities that are available.

An additional confounding issue is the fact that the majority of elderly Mexican Americans still prefer to speak their native language than to speak English. This is evidenced by the fact that the great majority, 87 percent, of the respondents in the survey that will be utilized for this analysis asked that the survey protocol be administered in Spanish. The issue of communication forces policy makers to look at how services are advertised, how programs are administered, how staffing patterns are determined, and, in general, the level of importance that effective communication with elderly Spanish-speaking Mexican Americans has as programs are developed, implemented, and evaluated.

To determine the use of services and family supports is also an important reason to study this group. Little is known about the elderly Mexican American as a consumer of institutional and community-based services. This lack of information sometimes leads policy makers to erroneously assume that no services are needed. Moreover, the predictable process of acculturation may create changes in the traditional family system.[18] These changes may impede the family network's ability to continue playing the role of caretaker of the elderly that researchers assumed it to have played.[19] There is considerable debate about this assumption given that there is no known data base that empirically supports the hypothesis of degree of familial support. Nevertheless, it is important to look at this group's perceptions and use of services in order to make policy recommendations that can address the future needs of these elders as potential consumers of long-term care.

Another aspect of the informal support system that has been documented and which complicates the interplay between the formal and informal systems is the fact that approximately 80 percent of the assistance that is provided to elderly people who live in the community is provided by the informal support network.[20] The fact that this level of assistance may be higher for the elderly Hispanics, given that they are disproportionately underrepresented in nursing homes, has not been researched with any definite conclusions.

This interplay between the formal and informal systems creates tension for policy planners and family advocates who see a need for evaluating future needs and planning for those needs. At the same time questions arise on the need to keep families intact and actively involved with their elders. Therefore, this study is important because studies have identified a variety of reasons within the characteristics of Hispanic elders which create barriers to service utilization.[21] However, there is little information available about characteristics of Hispanic elders and their service utilization which can contribute to policy development for this population.

SUMMARY

This study will look at levels of utilization of community-based services by different groups of elderly Hispanics. Further research will explore to what extent the frail (those experiencing two or more problems with Activities of Daily Living and at least one problem with Instrumental Activities of Daily Living and, or three or more ADL limitations and no IADL limitations, or four or more IADL limitations and no ADL limitations) elderly Mexican Americans use community-based formal services. In relation to this exploration, attention will be given to services that are being utilized and how the utilization compares among the Hispanic groups when the size of the informal support system is considered.

The Mexican American elderly will be the main focus of the research. However, given that the data provides a rare opportunity to explore similarities and differences among the three most populous ethnic groups, Mexican Americans, Cubans, and Puerto Ricans, some analyses will be offered on all three populations.

Analyses will also be completed on the elderly Mexican American sample to see if the data support the familism theory as the best descriptor of the behaviors that occur within the system. Additional information will be sought from current literature to see if the family system is expected to undergo a change as acculturation takes effect. Such a change would involve a move to the individual and his/her success and away from the family as the center of existence.

It is important to look at these issues given that the elderly Hispanic population is growing at a faster rate than other ethnic groups. Due to sheer increases in numbers and potential changes in the Hispanic family composition[22] planning for greater numbers of local community-based services will become more important in the future.

This section has set the context for the study on a subgroup of the elderly population that represents three percent of the total elderly in the United States population.

Notes

[1] GAO, 1992; Zsembik, 1994.

[2] Jose Cuellar, 1990, and The Commonwealth Fund Commission, 1989, found similar growth patterns.

[3] A projection of future increases in the 65 and over population is made by Hopper, 1993.

[4] The National Council of La Raza, 1990, and The Commonwealth Fund Commission, 1989, made growth projections to be between three to eight percent by 2020.

[5] Bassford, 1995, Pousada, 1995 and Zsembik, 1994, found that each Hispanic group is different from each other. The importance of this is a recent subject of research.

[6] Cuellar, 1990, and Marin and Marin, 1991, both discuss problems associated with generalizing applications of research findings to specific subgroups.

[7] Estrada, Trevino, and Ray, 1990, Henderson, 1993, and Zsembik, 1994, suggest that there are more differences among the subgroups than is generally known.

[8] Henderson, 1992, calls the differences "intra-cultural" variations.

[9] This finding comes from Weeks and Cuellar, 1981, who studied the role of family members with frail elders.

[10] Rumaldo Juarez, 1988, "Current and Future Long-Term Care Needs of Mexican American elderly in Arizona," In *Renato Rosaldo Lecture Series* 4 (1986-1987): 69-93.

[11] Congressional Budget Office, 1989, and Brian Gratton, 1987, both explored gender differences. This is also consistent with a widely-held view that older women are economically more disadvantaged.

[12] Brian Gratton, 1987; Rumaldo Juarez, 1986; James E. Lubben and Rosina M. Becerra, 1987, "El Barrio: Perceptions and Utilization of the Hispanic Neighborhood." In Steven R. Applewhite (Ed.), *The Hispanic Elderly in Transition.* Westport, CT: Greenwood Press: 135-141.

[13] This astonishingly high number has not changed dramatically since Rumaldo Juarez, 1986, addressed the Arizona high drop-out rate.

[14] Nationally the drop out-rate is consistently high per Barbara Kantrowitz and Lourdes Rosado, 1991.

[15] According to James C. Lubben and Rosina M. Becerra, 1987, the current Mexican American elder cohort is decidedly educationally disadvantaged since only 16 percent finished high school.

[16] Rumaldo Juarez, 1986; Eli Ginzberg, "Access to Health Care for Hispanics." *JAMA* 265 (1991).

[17] Maria E. Enchautegui, 1995, and Robert Greenstein, 1988, look at future socio-economic impacts of continued low educational achievement by the younger cohorts.

[18] How acculturation may change the traditional family system is unpredictable according to Lidia Pousada, 1995.

[19] The process of acculturation is a factor that Rosina M. Becerra, 1988, sees as possibly changing the caregiver role.

[20] The informal support network that Korbin Liu, Kenneth G. Manton, and Barbara Marzetta Liu, 1985, discuss includes unpaid individuals who provide assistance. This usually refers to family members, friends and other community members.

[21] Richard Chase, 1990, Michael Daley, 1989, and Fernando Trevino, M. Eugene Moyer, R. Burciaga Valdez and Christine A. Stroup-Benham, 1991, discuss several of these barriers.

[22] All of these studies (Bassford, 1995; GAO, 1992; Markides, Coreil, and Rogers, 1989) look at the increase of an elder population that will create different and new challenges to near-future program policy makers. These challenges will be similar to those created by all other racial and ethnic groups.

II

Literature Review

All societies develop definitions of illness that provide their
members with guidelines both for being ill and for responding
to illness.
Shanas and Maddox Handbook of Aging and the Social Sciences

All three major Hispanic groups will be studied in this work
although the thesis will focus on Mexican American elders. Within the
Hispanic population the Mexican American population is the largest
subgroup (62.3 percent) and also accounts for 54 percent of all elderly
Hispanics.[1] This section reviews the existing research on Mexican
American elders' use of community-based services, their use of informal
systems, and demographics that are detriments to their utilization of
service. The literature review is organized into three parts:

- Sociodemographics
- Primary/informal support system
- Utilization of formal support systems

SOCIODEMOGRAPHICS

This section presents descriptive data on elderly Hispanics that
provide a context for the current study. The first important characteristic
of this group concerns economic status. In 1988 Greenstein[2] wrote for the
Center on Budget and Policy Priorities in their report that Hispanics were
economically worse off than they had been in 1978. While the White and

African American poverty rates also increased during this period, they had grown by smaller margins. The White poverty rate grew from 8.7 percent to 10.5 percent (+1.2 percent), the African American poverty rate increased from 30.6 percent to 33.1 percent (+ 2.5 percent), and the Hispanic poverty rate increased 21.6 percent to 28.2 percent (+ 6.6 percent).

On August 27, 1991, *The Boston Globe*[3] carried similar statistics from the Children's Defense Fund. The report said that Hispanic children were becoming poor more quickly than either White or African American children. The Children's Defense Fund found that 33 percent of all Hispanic children were in poverty while 20 percent of all children in the United States lived in poverty in 1989. This information is of interest because it further supports the data that show poverty rates to be high among Hispanic families.

The Hispanic population as a whole is disproportionately represented in the lower economic strata,[4] and Hispanic elders are in the same predicament. Twenty-two percent of Hispanic elderly live in poverty compared with twelve percent of all elderly.[5] Elders are in the lower socioeconomic level because they have spent their lives in low-paying occupations.[6] As a result of being in seasonal and in the lowest paying jobs, they are also without medical insurance[7] and less likely to have financial resources from investments, accumulated savings, and other assets.[8]

Elderly Hispanic women are additionally less likely to have worked outside the home. Among those that did work for pay, two-thirds worked at unskilled, service-sector, or farm-sector jobs. This employment history adds credence to the theory of "multiple jeopardy" that has been applied to minority elderly. According to Gelfand (1982)[9] and Jackson (1970)[10] Hispanic elderly, like other ethnic elders, experienced a triple jeopardy of being old, minority, and poor. Additionally, Hispanic women also experienced sexism which is labeled a fourth jeopardy.

For elderly Hispanics the most common source of post-retirement income is Social Security.[11] Still, only 77 percent of the Hispanic elderly receive Social Security compared to 92 percent of all elderly.[12] Chase (1990)[13] found in his study that 66 percent of the Hispanic elders received Social Security and 4 percent received Supplemental Security Income. Given that Hispanic elders are disproportionately in poverty, the low rate of utilization of these programs is even more noteworthy.

Therefore, the effect of citizenship status on these utilization rates is explored in this study as much as possible given the data that is available.

PRIMARY SUPPORT SYSTEM

The primary support system (i.e., spouse, children, in-laws, grandchildren) of Mexican American elders has traditionally been credited with being a major factor in keeping them out of formal institutions and in the community. Underutilization of all services[14] is explained away by the belief that "they take care of their own." Although there is no research consensus on the strength of their primary social system[15] this thesis will look at the Mexican American family system as being an intergenerational, integrated system which continues to function as it had been historically depicted. This approach is used because more studies tend to support the theory about the strength of the family as the primary support system.

All Hispanic families, including Mexican Americans, Puerto Ricans, and Cubans, have traditionally been seen as systems that are interdependent and that encompass the extended family system. The Hispanic family system is characterized as placing high value on relatives as "referents and as providers of emotional support."[16] Familism, or familialism, thus is described as a socialization process whereby children are taught that the needs and welfare of the family, especially very old or very young family members, come first. This socialization process develops strong feelings of loyalty, pride, reciprocity, and solidarity among family members.[17]

Currently, no sociological theory applies, or has been applied, specifically, to Mexican American families. While the system of social reciprocity may be likened to George Homans' theory of social exchange, his theory was developed in work that looked at the behavior of majority culture subjects. The theory describes behavior that can be observed and quantified.[18] In Mexican American/Hispanic family systems, the application of this theory is limited because the theory does not consider the unquantifiable socialization process, inherent in the culture, which develops a feeling of oneness with family members. Unlike the majority culture, the familism system does not stress the success proposition, which has an individualistic and competitive orientation. For example, the culture does not emphasize tangible compensation for good deeds. In fact, the usual expression of gratitude includes the statement, *Que Dios te lo pague,* "May God reward you." When these words are spoken by an elder, they are both an expression of gratitude, as well as a blessing, and no worldly compensation is expected.

This socialization process establishes the lifelong patterns of behavior that will follow the Hispanic throughout his/her relationship with the family, and in many cases, with the majority culture. Nevertheless, how this plays out in the later life of the elders, and all Hispanics, in a majority culture that does not value such interdependence is not clear.[19]

Sociologists theorize that as societies move from the expressive (*Gesellschaft*) to the instrumental (*Gemeinschaft*) society, they become restricted or specialized and less generalized. Many Mexican Americans, in coming to the United States, moved from a rural life to an urbanized one and in the society of the United States, many human/familial activities have become compartmentalized.[20] Therefore, the traditional roles which are ascribed by the culture have changed and will continue to change as the Mexican American culture accedes to the majority culture.

In one of the first studies on elderly Mexican Americans, Carp (1968)[21] reported that children preferred to care and provide for elderly parents. She further stated that failure to do so constituted deviance among her informants. Crouch (1972)[22] found, however, that 61 percent of Mexican American elders thought that the family did not have an obligation to support them and only 38 percent stated that there was a familial responsibility for support. However, when asked whether the church, government, or the family had the greatest obligation to care for the elderly, 49 percent identified the family as having the greatest obligation. In Crouch's study only five percent said the government and a mere one percent said the church had the greatest responsibility to care for the elderly. Maldonado (1975)[23] had findings similar to those of Crouch in that 74 percent of his elderly sample also disagreed that older persons should live with their children. At the same time, 70 percent said that older people should live with persons their own age.

Weeks and Cuellar (1981)[24] found that although Hispanics have four times as many kin in close proximity compared to the other minority groups that they studied, Hispanics are less likely to turn to family members in time of need. As a matter of fact, when compared with six other minority groups, Hispanics were least likely to ask for help when they needed it. They preferred to be self-sufficient.

Mindel (1980), Gratton (1987), and Cantor (1985)[25] found that due to the cultural symbolism of the family, *la familia*, Mexican Americans do value and respect their elderly members. Sena-Rivera (1979)[26] agreed, contending that while the extended household has eroded in the United States because of social dislocation, belief and practice of *la familia* persists. His study suggests that geographic proximity is not a factor in the cultural norm of family values given that the belief persists in spite of the relocation of many Mexican Americans from Mexico to the United States and from rural to urban environments.

While the literature does not unilaterally support the familial theory over others, persistent findings appear in some significant areas. Many researchers (Bengston 1979; Dowd and Bengston 1978, Bastida 1979; Mindel 1980; and Greene and Monahan 1984)[27] have found that there is more interaction between Mexican American/Hispanic grandparents, children, and grandchildren than in African American or White families. There was also more of a social network for family members among the Hispanic groups than in either the White or African American respondents. Bastida (1979)[28] controlled for socioeconomic status and found that ethnic factors were better indicators of family integration. Her findings support the familial theory as an important part of the puzzle regarding the Hispanic family as a primary support system.

Markides et al. (1986)[29] found that although the elderly Mexican Americans were reluctant to ask for help from their children, the children provided necessary help. These findings suggest that frequent contact causes children to be more aware of the needs of the elders and, therefore, provide the help that is needed without being asked. This research supports the findings by Sena-Rivera (1979).[30]

This section has examined the role of the family within Mexican American and other Hispanic cultures. Previous research which shows the Hispanic family to be generationally integrated is also presented for future reference.

One of the issues for this researcher will be to develop a theory that is culturally appropriate to the Mexican American. It may be that the theory of "familism" is enough. In this case, a goal of the study will be to identify culturally relevant information on aspects of service provision that can be introduced as part of training packages for service providers. Culturally appropriate training of service providers is important because adult children of Hispanic elders have limited resources themselves and may simply be economically unable to care for their elders (Markides and Martin 1983; Chase 1990)[31] Conceivably, the formal system of the future at the local level of service delivery may play a greater role in the lives of Hispanic families. It is, therefore, the local level systems and not the state or federal bureaucracies that are addressed in this study.

The next section identifies issues concerning whether available services are utilized and, if so, at what levels. The paradox is also presented: should policy makers encourage greater utilization of services? If so, what impact might this have on the families that teach and value intergenerational dependence? And, finally, would the increased use of the formal support system hasten a process that would deny elders familial support, i.e., weaken the informal support system?

UTILIZATION OF FORMAL SUPPORT SYSTEM

The Commonwealth Fund Commission (1989)[32] completed the first analysis on this data set. They found that the most commonly used services by elderly Hispanics included going to a senior center (13 percent), eating meals at a senior center (13 percent), and utilizing transportation services (12 percent). These responses came from the 16 percent elderly Hispanics who had reported using one or more services in the last 12 months. However, of the 84 percent who had not used any services, 26 percent said they needed transportation services and 21 percent said they needed homemaker services. This discrepancy between service use and apparent unmet need for services needs to be better understood in spite of its complexity. Research is needed which will identify possible reasons for the discrepancies and where the discrepancies exist. Do the differences reflect a lack of available, needed services or unwillingness on the elders' part to use services?

Notes

[1] The National Council of La Raza 1991 has a policy section that researches issues related to elders of Latino backgrounds.

[2] Robert Greenstein compared the economic status of the three major groups in the United States and found that although all three groups were economically worse off, the Hispanics had lost by a larger percentage. This finding supports Rumaldo Juarez' concern for the younger Hispanic as a source of support for the elderly.

[3] *The Boston Globe*, 1991, reported the finding by the Children's Defense Fund that Hispanic children were becoming more poor more quickly than other children. Again this is critical information for policy makers to consider as family policies are developed.

[4] Trevino, Fernando M., M. Eugene Moyer, R. Burciaga Valdez, and Christine A. Stroup-Benham, 1991. "Health Insurance Coverage and Utilization of Health Services by Mexican Americans, Mainland Puerto Ricans, and Cuban Americans." *JAMA* (January 9th) 265 (2): 233-237.

[5] The report, *Poverty and Poor Health Among Elderly Hispanic Americans* 1989, is invaluable due to the comprehensive data that it makes available to program and policy makers.

[6] Jose Cuellar, 1990.

[7] See note 4 above.

[8] Kyriakos S. Markides and Harry W. Martin with Ernesto Gomez, 1983, provide data on the inability of Hispanic elders to save money due to low wages.

[9] See note 5 above.

[10] The "jeopardy theory" that Donald E. Gelfand, 1982, and James Jackson, 1970, discuss is an aging theory that is applicable to Hispanic elders.

[11] These researchers Kyriakos S. Markides and Harry W. Martin with Ernesto Gomez, 1983, as well as Richard A. Chase, 1990, support each others findings that Social Security income is the major source of post retirement for Hispanic elders.

[12] See note 5 above.

[13] The underutilization of Social Security and Supplemental Security Income by elderly Hispanics is documented by this researcher, Richard A. Chase, 1990.

[14] Benjamin Crouch, 1972, John Michael Daley, Steven R. Applewhite and James Jorquez, 1989, and Louise Woerner, 1979, provide support for their research of patterns of underutilizatin of services by Hispanic elders.

[15] The strength of the primary support system of Hispanic elders is discussed by Brian Gratton, 1987, David Maldonado, 1988, F. Penalosa, 1968, Josefina Estrada Velez, 1979, and Louise Woerner, 1979.

[16] How the Hispanic families view their interdependence on the extended family system is discussed by Geraldo Marin and Barbara VanOss Marin, 1991.

[17] The socialization process is discussed as a means of developing strong feelings for family members. According to Geraldo Marin, Barbara VanOss Marin 1991 and the National Council of La Raza, 1991, these feelings are the basis for the high value that is placed on the extended family.

[18] Ruth A. Wallace and Alison Wolf. *Contemporary Sociological Theory: Continuing the Classical Tradition* (1994; Englewood Cliffs, N.J.: Prentice-Hall, Inc.) 185-202.

[19] The dynamics of the interdependence that is learned and valued in Hispanic families is well documented but how this plays out in the

majority culture is not clear according to Marta Sotomayor and Steven R. Applewhite, 1988, 121-133.

[20] David Maldonado, 1988, 135-141 and Ana-Marie Rizzuto, 1981, 253-255 assert that traditional roles have changed in societies that go from an expressive to an instrumental social system.

[21] One of the earliest individuals to research the Mexican American family was Frances M. Carp, 1968.

[22] Benjamin Crouch, 1972, also found that younger family members see themselves as the caregivers. However, elders do not see this role as obligatory.

[23] See note 20 above.

[24] Family support systems may not be called upon by elders when help is needed according to John R. Weeks and Jose B. Cuellar, 1981, 388-394.

[25] Margaret Cantor, 1985, Brian Gratton, 1987, and Charles H. Mindel, 1980, found that elders are respected in their Mexican American families.

[26] Jaime Sena-Rivera, 1979, 121-129 also found that that in spite of an erosion of the extended family in the US, Mexican Americans continue to value the extended family.

[27] Elena Bastida, 1979, 42-49, Vern L. Bengston, 1979, James J. Dowd and Vern L. Bengston, 1978, 427-436, Vernon L. Greene and Deborah J. Monahan, 1984, 730-735, and Charles H. Mindel, 1980, 21-34 all found that there is more intergenerational interaction among Mexican American/Hispanic families than in African American or White families.

[28] Socioeconomic status appear to have less of an impact than ethnic factors when looking at family integration according to Elena Bastida, 1979, 42-49.

[29] Kyriakos S. Markides "Minority Status, Aging, and Mental Health," *International Journal of Aging and Human Development,* 285-300.

[30] See note 26 above.

[31] The idea that culturally appropriate services are necessary because of the economic disadvantage of families is discussed by Richard A. Chase, 1990, and Kyriakos S. Markides, Harry W. Martin with Ernesto Gomez, 1983.

[32] See note 5 above.

III

Methodology and Research Design

The proposed study is a secondary data analysis of the *Survey of Elderly Hispanics*, conducted by Westat, Inc., for the Commonwealth Fund Commission on Elderly People Living Alone. The data has been used by the Commission for its Final Report released in 1989.

This study will explore possible relations between elders who use community-based services and levels of frailty. This thesis posits that Hispanic elders access both the community-based, or formal, support system and the informal support system. Further, due to lack of evidence to the contrary, it may be that this interplay between these two important systems may facilitate frail Hispanic elders to stay in the community in spite of decreased functional capacity.[1] However, those Mexican American elders who negotiate access to formal support systems are more the exception than the norm.

Another area of study will be the informal support system that exists for both the Hispanic elders, frail and non-frail. Analysis will be completed on the frail elders and the size of the informal support system to examine any relations that may exist between the two.

SAMPLE

Background

The Survey of Elderly Hispanics is a random digit dialing selection of a sample of households. The screening was carried out in areas where there is a concentration of Hispanics. A community needed to have 30 percent Hispanic surnames in the telephone listings in order to be included in the sample. All of the screening and interviewing were carried out during August through October 1988. The survey was conducted as an extension of the 1986 National Survey on Problems Facing Elderly Americans Living Alone and was designed to investigate specific problems of the elderly Hispanic population. The survey was conducted in two stages. The first stage was the screener and the second was the telephone interview.

Screener

The screener stage consisted of a questionnaire that was designed to be administered over the telephone to self identified Hispanic persons who were 65 years or older. In the screening phase the telephone number was the sample unit. The households that were to be screened were selected via random digit dialing from telephone exchanges that had 30 percent Hispanic households.

Approximately 48,000 households were telephoned and asked if the household was Hispanic, and if a person or persons over 65 years of age lived in the home. If more than one elderly Hispanic person resided in the household, all were asked to participate. Bilingual interviewers were available and 87 percent of the respondents asked to have the interview completed in Spanish.

Telephone Interview

Telephone interviewing was used as the means of data collection. Since the Census Bureau data indicates that approximately 92 percent of the elderly Hispanics have telephones,[2] the restriction of the interviewing method did not seriously affect the quality of the data.

Sample Design

Three alternative sampling frames were considered for conducting the survey. The random digit dialing was selected due to various aspects of data quality. However, two major problems that had to be dealt with were:

1. Locating and identifying enough elderly Hispanics. Because Hispanic elders are a rare group in the U. S. (in 1988 there were 900,000) this means that large numbers of households have to be screened in order to find the desired sample. For example, to get a sample of 370 Puerto Ricans, 370,000 households had to be screened. Therefore, the sample design had to be constructed in a manner that would be financially feasible but still produce a representative sample.

2. Attaining the desired sample sizes for the four Hispanic subgroups. If a uniform sample size throughout the United States had been used, more Mexican American elderly would have been in the sample and fewer Puerto Rican American and Cuban Americans. Therefore, the sample design was developed to be responsive to the needed sample size of the four subgroups.

Problem one was handled by using computer tapes that contain housing and population statistics for all the telephone exchanges in the country. Those exchanges that contained 30 percent Hispanics were identified. The sample was then restricted to these exchanges. Within the selected exchanges, a random sample of households were selected with random digit dialing. Therefore, every household that had a telephone in the exchange had an equal chance of selection and screening requirements were dramatically reduced.

The second problem was handled by dividing the U. S. into three geographic areas.

1. New England and the Middle Atlantic states which are the northeastern states up to and including New Jersey and Pennsylvania,

2. Florida; and,

3. The remainder of the U. S.

This scheme was designed to capture primarily Puerto Ricans in the first group, Cubans in the second group, and Mexican Americans in the third group. Sampling rates were set in each geographic area to provide the desired number of elders. No particular sampling rate was set for the fourth category of "Other Hispanics." They were found during the screening process. Although each geographic area was specifically used to obtain a specific targeted population, if a member of another subgroup was identified during the screening process, they were included in the sample. Consequently, members of all four groups were collected into the sample regardless of geographic area of residence.

HYPOTHESES

Researchers have so far been unable to ascertain the relation between community-based elders' frailty level and their utilization of informal and formal supports. One of the purposes of the following exploratory study is to generate hypotheses which can be further explored in future research. This study proposes to answer the following seven research questions:

1. Those Mexican American elders who utilize the greatest number of formal services will also be the elder who are frail.

2. The more children who live within one hour from the Mexican American elder, the less likely that the elder will utilize community-based services.

3. As a whole, this sample of Mexican Americans will be similar to previous Mexican American study samples. These elders will have fewer financial resources and more self-identified health problems.

4. Verbal English language skills are positively related to utilization of community-based services.

5. The size of the family informal support network has a significant influence on the ability of Hispanic elders to remain in the community even when health and financial status are controlled.

6. Ethnicity is a predictor of different rates of use of service utilization among Mexican Americans, Cubans, and Puerto Ricans.

7. There will be differences in the sample population based on gender. These differences will be in the areas of income, education, and number of formal services utilized. The men will have higher incomes and levels of education. The women will have higher rates of use of community-based services.

METHODOLOGICAL APPROACH

Plan of Analysis

The analytic plan for this study consists of three stages. First, univariate statistics, frequencies and measures of central tendency, are presented for each of the independent and dependent variables. The second stage examines the bivariate relations between the dependent and independent variables. For interval level data and dummy variables, association levels are shown by using Pearson's Correlation Coefficients; crosstabs are used for nominal and ordinal data and t-test results are presented to show the significance of the association between variables.

The Mexican American, Puerto Rican, and Cuban populations are the groups examined in this section of analysis. The "Other" category of Hispanics could not be disaggregated to provide information on the different ethnic groups as the sample numbers were not greater than 50. Therefore, the analysis will include only the three aforementioned groups.

Although the focus of the thesis is the Mexican America sample population, the data set offers a unique opportunity to explore similarities and differences among the different Hispanic subgroups. This type of study has seldom been possible with previous data due to the small numbers of the subgroups and/or due to the grouping of all subgroups into the Hispanic category.

The third stage utilizes multiple regression techniques to test the hypothesis that the Mexican American elderly population utilizes community-based services at significantly different rates than the other two elder groups. Among utilizers of community-based services, I will explore the relations that exist between the dependent variable, total number of community-based services used, and independent variables.

VARIABLES USED IN THE STUDY

Sociodemographic and Individual Characteristics

Variable	*Description*
AGE	Age variable that is continuous and ranges from 65 to 100 years.

ETHNICITY   Nominal data that denotes the ethnicity of the three groups:

> 1 = Mexican Americans
> 2 = Cuban Americans
> 3 = Puerto Ricans

INCOME   A continuous variable for income in increments of $5,000.

EDUC   A continuous variable for years of schooling.

GENDER   A dummy variable that takes on the value of "1" if the respondent is a male, "0" if female.

INSUR   A dummy variable that takes the value of "1" if the respondent receives Medicare, Medicaid, or has other insurance, "0" otherwise.

MARITAL   A dummy variable that takes on a value of "1" if the respondent is married, "0" otherwise.

SPEAK   A dummy variable that takes on the value of "1" if the respondent speaks English, "0" otherwise.

MCAID A dummy variable that takes on a value of "1" if the respondent receives Medicaid, "0" otherwise.

Informal Support System

WTHSSUP (LIVE WITH SOMEONE)	A continuous variable that was constructed from the sum of the six questions when the respondent's response indicated a positive informal support, (s)he received a point. The six dichotomous variables are:
v24	An elder receives a "1" if (s)he lives with a spouse, "0" otherwise.
v25	A "1" indicates that the respondent lives with a child, "0" otherwise.
v26	A respondent receives a "1" if (s)he lives with siblings, "0" otherwise.
v27	A value of "1" indicates if the elder lives with his/her parents, "0" otherwise.
v28	A "1" indicates that the elder lives with other relatives, "0" otherwise.
v29	An elder receives a "1" if the elder lives with friends, "0" otherwise.
CHDN	An interval level variable for number of children the elder has.
TIME	An interval level variable for "time child arrives" to the elder's home which ranges from 1 to 120 minutes.
CHIDAY	"Sees kids often" is a nominal variable converted to a dummy variable. The value is "1" if the respondent saw the child at least once per day, "0" otherwise.
CHIWK	"Sees kids often" was converted to a dummy variable and the value is "1" if the respondent saw the child at least once per week, "0" otherwise.

INFRMSS   A dummy variable that takes the value of "1" if the respondent was cared for by a family member or spouse or a friend or neighbor after (s)he left the hospital.

NOCARE   A dummy variable that takes on the value of "1" if the respondent did not need care after (s)he left the hospital, "0" otherwise.

SELFCARE   A dummy variable that takes on the value of "1" if the respondent cared for self after (s)he left the hospital, "0" otherwise.

Level of Frailty Domain

FRAIL   This dummy variable was constructed and given a value of "1" if a respondent had identified him/herself as having difficulty with two or more Activities of Daily Living *and* one or more Instrumental Activities of Daily Living limitations, or with three or more Activities of Daily Living and no IADL limitations, or with four or more Instrumental Activities of Daily Living and no ADL limitations, "0" otherwise.

TOTADL   This is a continuous variable ranging from 1 to 7. It was constructed from the sum of the questions measuring limitations with Activities of Daily Living The Activities of Daily Living include the following dichotomous variables:

    v73   Difficulty bathing or showering?

    v83   Difficulty in dressing?

    v93   Difficulty eating?

    v103   Difficulty getting in or out of bed or chairs?

v113   Difficulty walking?

v123   Difficulty getting outside?

v133   Difficulty using the toilet, including getting to the toilet?

TOTIADL   A continuous variable constructed from the six questions measuring difficulties with Instrumental Activities of Daily Living. These questions included the following dichotomous variables:

v143   Difficulty preparing your own meals?

v153   Difficulty managing your money (includes activities such as keeping track of expenses and paying bills).

v163   Difficulty using the telephone?

v173   Difficulty with shopping for personal items (such as toilet items or medications).

v183   Difficulty with heavy housework (includes activities such as scrubbing floors or washing windows).

v193   Difficulty with light housework (such as doing dishes, straightening up or light cleaning).

HLTHPROB   A dummy variable constructed if 1) doctor visits were more than 13 per year, or 2) if the respondent retired for health reasons, or 3) if the respondent answered "yes" to having stayed in the hospital overnight within the last twelve months, or 4) if the respondent described his/her health as "poor", "0" otherwise.

HOSP   A dummy variable that takes on the value of "1" if the respondent has been a patient overnight in a hospital during the past twelve months, "0" otherwise.

POORHLTH   A dummy variable that takes on the value of "1" if the respondent said that his/her health, in general, was poor, "0" otherwise.

DRVISITS   An interval level variable that gives information on how many times the respondent saw a medical doctor or a doctor's assistant during the past twelve months.

Formal Support System

FORSYS   A dummy variable that takes on the value of "1" if the respondent was cared for by a home health agency, a private nurse, or a nursing home after (s)he left the hospital, "0" otherwise.

TOTCBS   A continuous variable constructed from ten questions which measured community based services which are used by the respondents. The potentially used community-based services are the following dichotomous variables:

    v251   Use transportation for the elderly?

    v252   Use a senior center?

    v253   Have meals delivered to your home by an agency or organization like Meals on Wheels?

    v254   Eat meals in a senior center or in some place with a special meal program for the elderly?

    v255   Use homemaker services for the elderly that provides services like cleaning and cooking in the home?

    v256   Use a service which makes routine telephone calls to check on the health of elderly people?

v257   Use a visiting nurse service?

v258   Use a home health aide who comes into the home?

v259   Use food stamps or coupons?

v260   Use services or programs for the elderly provided by
your church?

LIMITATIONS OF THE DATA

A major limitation of the data is incomplete information about
respondents' location. The dependent variable measures total community-
based services used (TOTCBS) and formal support systems (FORSYS)
used and how they may be impacted by the geographic region of each
respondent. Regional information is important since each state has
slightly different definitions of what constitutes frailty, i.e., functional and
cognitive limitations. Since the definitions shape access to services, the
availability of community-based services differs accordingly.
Additionally, there is disparity in availability of services as well as
eligibility criteria for services across states. This may be less true for
Medicare than for the community-based services. There is even variation
within the states from county to county. According to Harel et al. (1987),[3]
"The extent to which benefits and services may be available for ethnic
aged may vary considerably in different locations."

An additional complication is that the ethnic participants are not
identified with a certain state or region. As has been explained, although
Puerto Ricans are primarily found in the Northeast region, they also live
in other states throughout the United States. Consequently, the findings
from this research would have been more precise, if the exact state-of-
origin information of each of the participants were available for these
analyses. The same dilemma applies to the other two ethnic groups.
Would a Puerto Rican in New Mexico be as likely to use community-
based services as one in New Jersey? And what role would the
differences of available services in the different states play in the different
use of services if, in fact, there was a difference?

The data are also limited with respect to informal support. While it is acknowledged that, "the informal support system is of central importance in the lives of all elderly, including the lives of ethnic aged"[4] previous research has not reached a consensus on how this important system assists the frail Hispanic elders to remain in their communities. Likewise, these data are limited with respect to shedding light on the nature and effects of informal supports. However, given the attention that these populations are recently receiving, future researchers are likely to define some of the answers in qualitative and quantitative research.

Finally, the data collected in this survey do not include level of intensity of functional and cognitive limitations. Some researchers[5] have addressed the need to define level of intensity to determine a more precise measurement for frailty. However, given that the data collected did not explore that level of definition, the research for this paper will be constrained by the data that is available.

THEORETICAL FRAMEWORK

"The informal support system is of central importance in the lives of all elderly, including in the lives of ethnic aged. This support system includes children, family members, friends and neighbors" (p 202).[6]

Previous research has compared the use of health services by Hispanic rates of utilization by the majority elderly population. Much of this research has led to conclusions that elderly Hispanics, as well as other Hispanic age groups, use services at a different rate than elderly Whites.[7] Additionally, the comparisons have primarily been limited to uses of community health services. While continuing this discourse is important, this is not the focus of this research.

However, it is important to note two recent studies that explore the role that ethnicity plays in service utilization. O'Sullivan and Lasso (1992) found that Hispanics underutilized private mental health services when compared to Anglos. Their findings also suggest that in the public care arena, there are no ethnic differences in utilization of services. This finding is not supported by Moore and Hepworth (1994)[8] who explored the use of perinatal and infant health services by Mexican American and White, non-Hispanic mothers who were Medicaid enrollees. Although the research was not based on similar health care issues (mental health and infant health services) nor with elders. These differing results suggest that the definitive answer to the role that ethnicity plays in service utilization has not yet been found.

The current study delves into utilization of services by other groups and proposes to compare the rate of utilization of community-based services by the three elderly Hispanic groups–Mexican Americans, Cuban Americans, and Puerto Ricans. The community-based services include: transportation for the elderly, senior centers, meal delivery, special meal programs, homemaker services, telephone checks, visiting nurse services, home health aide, food stamps, and elderly programs provided by a church. This list is unique because it includes a few health services as well as social services and one service that is an entitlement program.

No current research explores the use of this mixture of community-based services by the three Hispanic groups. However, there is some discussion on the heterogeneity among the different Hispanic groups. This research explores various theoretical explanations for the differential use of community-based services by these three groups. Some of the explanations that have been suggested for the heterogeneity include:

> Patterns of immigration to the United States–how and why each group came to this country–may be factors that create different utilization patterns.[9]

> Education levels of immigrant groups vary and this plays a role in the way services are viewed and utilized by group members.[10]

> The different political and social systems of their countries of origin created different values, expectations, and behaviors.[11]

> Differential access to health care in earlier years.[12]

> Differential labor force participation and its subsequent role in health status later in life.[13]

There is limited literature that addresses the use of community-based services as described in this research. Neither is there a comparison by the three groups of use of these identified services. However, some studies suggest approaches to increase the rate of utilization of some of these services by these groups. For example, Starrett. et al. (1990),[14] suggests that one way to improve the utilization is to provide bilingual public information on the services that are available in each specific community.

This data set did not allow for conclusive evidence regarding the various theoretical explanations. However, some valuable findings are reported. These findings can be used to build future research models. The next chapter discusses these findings.

Notes

[1] Korbin Liu, Kenneth G. Manton and Barbara Marzetta Liu, 1985, found that Hispanic elders are more likely to have a higher level of frailty and remain in the community.

[2] The Commonwealth Fund Commission (Baltimore, MD: The Commonwealth Fund Commission, 1989).

[3] Zev Harel, Ed McKinney and Michael Williams, 1987, found the differences that occur between states. It is possible that this is due to the political climate of each state as well as the economy of each state.

[4] Harel, McKinney and Williams, 1987, 202.

[5] Lois M. Verbrugge, James M. Lepkowski, and Yuichi Imanaka, 1989, suggest that researchers factor in the intensity of limitations to truly measure frailty.

[6] Harel, McKinney, and Williams, 1987, 202.

[7] Michael J. O'Sullivan and Bethsabe Lasso "Community Mental Health Services for Hispanics: A Test of the Culture Compatibility Hypothesis," *Hispanic Journal of Behavioral Sciences* (1992), 455-468. Claudia L. Schur, Leigh Ann Albers and Mark L. Berk "Extended Kinship in the United States: Competing Models and the Case of La Familia Chicana," *Health Care Financing Review* (1995), 71-88.

[8] Patricia Moore and Joseph T. Hepworth, 1994, hypothesized that if both populations were on Medicaid, the rate of health care utilization would be similar irrespective of ethnicity.

[9] Carmela G. Lacayo, Jean K. Crawford, Henry Rodriguez and Ramona Soto, 1980, explored the differential rates of utilization.

[10] Two groups of researchers (Antonio L. Estrada, Fernando M. Trevino and Laura A. Ray, 1991, and Julia M. Solis, Gary Marks, Melinda Garcia and David Shelton, 1991) have researched the role of education levels that immigrants bring with them and subsequent use of services.

[11] See note 9 above as well as Woerner, 1979.

[12] Kyriakos S. Markides, Harry W. Martin with Ernesto Gomez *Older Mexican Americans: A Study in An Urban Barrio* (1983; Austin, TX: The Center for Mexican American Studies of the University of Texas at Austin).

[13] See note 11 above.

[14] Richard A. Starrett, Charles Bresler, James T. Decker, Gary T. Walters and Dan Rogers, 1990, studied the environmental awareness of the Hispanic elderly.

IV

Research Findings

INTRODUCTION

This chapter reports the results of the descriptive and bivariate statistical procedures that were used to analyze the data. The sample included 937 Mexican Americans, 714 Cuban Americans, and 368 Puerto Ricans. The total of the elderly Hispanic groups is 2,019. As might be expected, the number of respondents for some of the questions were less than the full sample of 2,019. As previously mentioned, none of the "Other" ethnic groups were considered since none had a sample size of more than 50 respondents.

The first section reports the univariate analyses of the dependent and independent variables, setting the context for the rest of the analyses. These descriptors, including demographic data, number of ADL limitations, number of IADL limitations, and total number of community-based services used, provide the basic data necessary for a comprehensive understanding of the three Hispanic elder populations.

The second section presents the bivariate relations between the different independent variables and the three ethnic groups, including an analysis of whether and how elderly Mexican Americans who are frail use community-based services. Additionally, the relations and differences among the three different ethnic groups will be discussed, illustrating important demographic differences.

DESCRIPTION OF THE SAMPLE

Univariate and Bivariate Descriptions of the Hispanic Elders:

The elders who responded to this survey were 65 years or older in 1987, the year for which the data were collected. In this sample, the average age was 73.5 years. Additionally, elders in the sample had an average 6.6 years of formal education. (However, elders in the most frequently identified educational category, were likely to have completed only three years of formal education.)

Of the elders who had children (245 respondents had no children), the average number of children was four (see table 4.1).

Though these elders have lived in the United States for an average of 36 years, those who do not speak good or excellent English are in the majority with 72 percent of the 2019 elders in this category. If the data are examined for how many speak any English, 50 percent (n = 1724) say that they do. These findings are consistent with Frances Carp's (1968)[1] statement, "Many Mexican-Americans speak or read little or no English and understand little of it" (p 4).

It is three times as likely that elders in this sample live with someone else (75 percent), than by themselves. Of the 2019, 955 or 47 percent live with a spouse, and 697 or 35 percent live with a child. Of these elders, some live with both spouse and child.

Table 4.1

Summary of various
Socio-demographic descriptive statistics

Variable	Mean	Standard Deviation
Age (n = 2,019)	73.5	6.801
Number of Children (n = 1,771)	4	2.834
HH Income/year (n = 1,330)	$10,800	1.325
Time Child gets to Elder's Home minutes (n = 1,004)	12.6	12.441
Years of Formal Education	6	4.264
Total ADL Limitations (n = 2,019)	1.1	1.783
Total IADL Limitations (n = 2,019)	1.2	.036
Total Community- Based Service (n = 2,019)	1.1	.031

Because these data were collected in 1988, 1987 is the year for which total household income data was collected with this survey. The income question had the fewest respondents, with only 1,330 or 68 percent of the 2,019 answering this question.

Elders in this sample had a mean annual income of $10,800. However, this is deceptive because, in fact, a large portion (525 or 26 percent) of the sample had incomes of $5,500 or less. This represents the lowest income category. Only 54 respondents (4 percent) earned $35,000 and over. According to Marin and Marin (1991)[2], the median income for Hispanic families in 1987 was $20,306. Thus the median income for elders is 60 percent of the median family income for Hispanic families. During this same year, 26 percent of all Hispanic families had incomes below the poverty line.

For the elders with children, the average time it takes for children to get to the elders' house is 13 minutes. The mode is five minutes with 176 elders identifying this time. Therefore, it appears that the average elder lives very close to his/her children. Amazingly, 99.8 percent of the elders with children have children within 60 minutes and 50 percent (1,015) have children within 10 minutes. This latter figure includes all the elders who live with their children, which is 697.

The next area of the research includes the data which describe the elders' health. Fourteen percent or 284 individuals described their health as "excellent" and 11 percent or 230 said their health was "poor." The majority of the respondents, 1,490 (74 percent of n = 2,004), said their health was good or fair (see table 4.2).

Table 4.2

Self reported health status
(n = 2,019)

Health Status	Number	Percent
Excellent	284	14.1
Good	644	31.9
Fair	846	41.9
Poor	230	11.4
(Missing)	15	.7

Interestingly, more than twice as many are considered frail[3] (n = 517) as reported themselves to be in poor (n = 230) health. This could mean that the categories[4] which are used to classify people as eligible for nursing homes result in outcomes which are very different from the way Hispanics view themselves.

Because of this finding, elders and their total number of identified functional limitations or activities of daily living were examined. Sixty-two percent (n = 1,248) needed no assistance with ADL limitations and 13 percent (260) needed assistance with only one ADL. Only 511 of these elders (n = 2,019) needed assistance with two or more ADL limitations; but 57 needed assistance with six ADL limitations and 42 needed assistance with all seven ADL limitations. Thus, five percent of the sample experiences extreme difficulties in their lives yet manages to remain in the community (see table 4.3). In the analysis, "eating" was difficult for the smallest number (5.3 percent), while "walking" presented difficulty to the most respondents (27.3 percent) (see table 4.4).

Table 4.3

Number and percentage of problems with
ADL limitations and IADL limitations experienced by respondents
(n = 2,019)

Number	Activities of daily living			Instrumental activities of daily living		
0	1,248	=	61.8%	946	=	46.9%
1	260	=	12.9%	508	=	25.2%
2	182	=	9.0%	208	=	10.3%
3	95	=	4.7%	119	=	5.9%
4	69	=	3.4%	87	=	4.3%
5	66	=	3.3%	77	=	3.8%
6	57	=	2.8%	74	=	3.7%
7	42	=	2.1%			

Table 4.4

Activities of daily living difficulty by total respondents

ADL	Number	Percent	Std. Err.
Bathing or showering	297	14.7	.008
Dressing	233	11.5	.007
Eating	107	5.3	.005
Getting in and out of bed or chairs	423	21.0	.009
Walking	552	27.3	.010
Getting outside	390	19.3	.009
Using toilet, including getting to the toilet	149	7.4	.006
Total	2,458[1]	38.2	

[1]Some respondents identified multiple ADL limitations. Therefore, the total 2,458 is greater than 2,019.

As might be expected, the difficulty in walking affects other ADL limitations that involve mobility. For example, difficulty with "getting in and out of bed" was experienced by 21 percent, and with "getting out of the house" by 19.3 percent of the respondents.

Because there is no universal definition of frail the author developed her own. The definition includes having difficulty with at least two ADL limitations *and* one or more IADL limitations, or three or more ADL limitations and no IADL limitations, or four or more IADL limitations and no ADL limitations. This second definition is more representative of different definitions that currently abound in the literature and that are used by states to determine whether an elder is eligible for nursing home placement. Nursing home placement is based on different definitions of frailty. In Appendix A, the four states that were examined by Jackson et al. 1991,[5] are included as examples of how different states define frailty.

A strong argument for the expansion of the definition is to make the results more generalizable. Originally, the definition of frail was operationalized as having two ADL limitations and having one or more IADL limitations. Given this definition, the number of frail respondents was 475. However, once frail was defined as more inclusive, it was very interesting that only 42 more individuals (nine percent) were added to the FRAIL category. Therefore, the total sample of individuals defined as frail is 517.

Furthermore, of the elderly population in the analysis of total instrumental activities of daily living, 946 respondents (46 percent) needed no assistance with any instrumental activities of daily living. Five hundred and eight respondents needed assistance with only one instrumental activity of daily living while at the other end of the spectrum, 77 respondents identified themselves as needing assistance with five instrumental activities of daily living and 74 respondents needed assistance with all six instrumental activities of daily living. A total of 7.5 percent of the total sample needed assistance with five or six instrumental activities of daily living. The most frequently identified difficulty with instrumental activities of daily living was doing heavy housework. The two instrumental activities of daily living that they experienced the least difficulty with were managing money (11.4 percent) and using the telephone (11.6 percent) (see table 4.5).

Table 4.5

Frequency of problems with instrumental activities of daily living
difficulty by total respondents

IADL	Number	Percent	Std. Dev.
Preparing your own meals	316	15.7	.363
Managing your money	230	11.4	.318
Using the telephone	234	11.6	.320
Shopping for personal items	404	20.0	.400
Doing heavy housework	963	47.7	.500
Doing light housework	311	15.4	.361
Total	2,458[1]		

[1]Some respondents identified multiple IADL limitations. Therefore, the total 2,458 is greater than the sample.

Correspondingly, the total community-based services that are utilized were also examined. Nine hundred twenty-one respondents (47 percent) do not use any of the listed services. As seen in tables 4.6 and 4.7, another 517 (25 percent) use one service. Given that the majority (72 percent) of the elders use zero or one community service, only 28 percent of this population can be described as using a "high" number of community-based services. (Some of these figures differ from the *Report of the Commonwealth Fund Commission on Elderly People Living Alone,* (1989)[6] due to the selection of the three Hispanic groups.)

Table 4.6

Total community-based services used by all respondents[1]

Value	Frequency	Percent
0	921	45.6
1	517	25.6
2	283	14.0
3	165	8.2
4	71	3.5
5	35	1.7
6	20	1.0
7	4	.2
8	2	.1
9	1	.0

[1]Standard Error = .031
Mean = 1.09 The average for the community-based services used by all of the frail elders is 5.83. In contrast, those who are not frail use 5.33.

Table 4.7

Noted use of different community-based services

Service Used	Number of Responses	Yes	Percent Yes
Senior Transportation	2,015	300	14.9
Senior Center	2,016	261	12.9
Meals on Wheels	2,018	122	6.0
Senior Meals	2,015	276	13.7
Homemaker Service	2,018	155	7.7
Phone Checks	2,013	81	4.0
Visiting Nurses	2,018	219	10.9
Home Health Service	2,015	105	5.2
Food Stamps	2,017	572	28.4
Senior Church Program	2,013	119	5.9

The number of visits to a doctor among the respondents (n = 1,297) provides an interesting perspective on the use of medical services. The mean is seven visits per year. There were 181 people (14 percent) who did not go to any doctor during the year. Conversely, as seen in table 4.8, there were some individuals who went a total of 75 to 260 times per year to see a doctor.

Table 4.8

Frequency of visits to a doctor
by respondents*

Value[1,2]	Frequency	Valid %
0	181	14.0
0 - 5	749	57.7
7 - 11	225	12.2
13 - 17	42	3.2
18 - 23	43	3.4
24 - 30	84	6.4
32 - 44	18	1.4
45 - 60	14	1.2
75 - 120	5	.5
144 - 260	4	.4

[1]The values were not sequential.
[2]722 (35.8%) were missing
*Std. Error = 14.94

Those 479 elders (24 percent) who said they had been in the hospital for an overnight stay during the past twelve months were queried on who had provided care post hospital stay. The majority (371) were cared for by a spouse, child, friend, or neighbor, i.e., the informal support system. Sixty-one (three percent of the total sample) were cared for by the formal system, which in this series of questions is defined as a home health agency, private nurse, or nursing home.

Summary

These findings support studies done by Lacayo (1980), Marin and Marin (1991)[7] and others on the socio-demographic characteristics of elderly Hispanics. This sample is comparable to other samples of elderly Hispanics, justifying the generalizations which may be drawn from the multivariate analyses.

A review of the descriptive analyses presents a population of elderly Hispanics where the majority speak Spanish, live with someone else, and are less likely to consider themselves as being in poor health. Those who experience activities of daily living limitations have more problems with mobility functions. These limitations may impact the area of instrumental activities of daily living limitations where the greatest percentage of problems are with "doing heavy housework." As a group, this sample of elders used few community-based services.

BIVARIATE ANALYSES

Introduction

This section presents the results of the bivariate analyses. In each instance the analyses are presented for the total population and then for the three Hispanic groups. The total Mexican American sample includes 937 respondents; the Cuban American sample has 714, and the Puerto Rican sample has 368 participants. The analysis of variance found that Cuban Americans are the oldest with a mean age of 73.93, the Mexican Americans are close behind with a mean age of 73.46, and the youngest are the Puerto Ricans with a mean age of 72.95 ($p = .001$).

Total number community-based services utilized by high service use

The results of the analysis of variance on the total community-based services that are utilized by the three Hispanic elderly groups reflect a statistically significant difference ($p < .001$) in services used. The data suggest differences in the use of community-based services for different groups. For example, the average community-based services used by the total 2,019 respondents is 1.09, but males use .86 services and females use 1.23 ($F = .762$; $p < .0001$). The results are based on 738 male respondents and 1,281 female respondents.

Perhaps the biggest surprise in the results was the fact that the respondents who do not speak English access more community-based services than those who do ($p < .05$). Those who do not speak English use 1.14 community-based services and the English-speaking Hispanic elders use 0.98. The English-speaking elders use fewer services than the total average 1.09 for all the respondents.

There are 566 respondents (28 percent of the total sample) who speak English. Interestingly, 87 percent of the respondents had requested that the questionnaire be administered in Spanish, yet 72 percent of the sample speak only Spanish. While small, this 15 percent difference suggests that if given a choice, many English-speaking Hispanic elders prefer to speak in their native language.

Who uses community-based services and at what functional and cognitive level are important questions. Therefore, analyses were completed on the sample to explore the use of community-based services depending on the limitations in the activities of daily living and instrumental activities of daily living.

In this section the definition of high use of community-based services (HIUSE) is two or more services. This definition is used because 1438 (71.2 percent) of the sample population use zero or one service (see table 4.6). The literature did not yield definitions of high and low utilization. As is seen in table 4.3, if high use were defined more conservatively, the subset of high users would be very small.

Those 62 respondents identified as high users used an average of 5.61 community-based services. Per the ANOVA results, the 1957 individuals who did not fall into the "high users" category used only 0.95

community-based services per respondent (p < .001). Furthermore, the 62 respondents who are high users of services, fall into both frail and non-frail groups. However, the average number of community-based services used by frail elders is 1.61. In contrast, those who are not frail use 0.92.

Of the 517 elders who are frail, it is interesting that only 35 are high users of community-based services. These frail elders use 5.61 services. The remaining 482 who are frail use 1.30 services. Therefore, the average use of services is 1.61 community-based services for all the frail respondents. The data indicate that the majority of frail Hispanic elders are not high users of services (p < .001). Nonetheless, as seen in table 4.9 those who are frail do use more services than the non-frail and the difference is significant (p < .001).

Table 4.9

Analysis of variance results for selected variables
total community-based services used
(Mean)

High use by frail[*]	5.61 (n = 35)
High use by non-frail[*]	5.33 (n = 27)
Frail not high use[*]	1.30 (n = 482)
Not frail[*] Not high use	0.84 (n = 1475)

[*]p < .001

In analyzing high use by gender, over three times as many women as men use five or more services. There were 47 women and 15 men in the high users category.

Those who are not frail but are high users use 5.33 services per person. On the other hand, those who are frail and are high users, use 5.61 services per respondent. A very interesting finding is that far more frail elders are low users (n = 482) than are high users of services (n = 35) (see table 4.10). These findings are counter intuitive and do not support the hypotheses.

Another factor of interest is how level of income relates to the number of community-based services used. Respondents with incomes under $15,000 per year use 1.16 (n = 1826) community-based services per person. Those with incomes over $15,000 per year (n = 193) use 0.51 community-based service. These data show that people with higher income utilize very few community-based services. This may suggest that stigma is a factor in service utilization. Some elders may associate using government provided services with the "welfare" system. Elderly Hispanics with high incomes may feel that the community-based services are targeted for low-income people and that the services are inferior to what can be purchased. A second reason for not using these services is that the elders may perceive them as charity.

Although this research explored level of frailty from a combination of functional and cognitive limitations, it was important to make independent analyses of each area of limitations to contribute to existing data. Therefore, the next two areas of analyses present the analytic results.

Functional Limitations

In looking at the functional difficulties that the respondents experienced, it was found that the total population experienced limitations in 1.07 activities of daily living. The respondents who are frail report having almost four (3.58) functional limitations. The ANOVA findings show that those who are not frail report having 0.20 functional limitations. In looking at the frail males and females there are a total of 141 frail men and 376 frail females. The chi-square shows a significant relation between being frail and gender of respondents at the p < .0001 level.

Cognitive Limitations

The cognitive limitations were examined in relation to ethnicity and being frail. It is interesting that more cognitive limitations (n = 1.22) than functional limitations were noted across all three ethnic groups. As with the functional limitations, the difference in number of cognitive limitations between the non-frail and the frail was significant (p < .001) (see tables 4.10 and 4.11).

The total population reports 1.22 IADL limitations. In comparing the frail versus the non-frail respondents, the frail report 3.27 IADL limitations and the non-frail report 0.51 IADL limitations.

In looking at the gender differences, females experienced 1.37 IADL limitations and men reported 0.95. It appears that females are more impaired (p < .001). The analysis of variance also supports significant differences in the frail and non-frail men and in the frail and non-frail women (p < .001) as related to their cognitive limitations.

Table 4.10

Analysis of variance results for frail elders by ADL and IADL limitations

	FRAIL (Mean)	NOT FRAIL (Mean)
No. ADL Limitations[*]	3.58 (n = 517)	0.20 (n = 1502)
No. IADL Limitations[*]	3.27 (n = 517)	0.51 (n = 1502)

[*]p < .001

Table 4.11

Mean number of reported
ADL limitations
and IADL limitations
by gender

	Males (Mean)	Females (Mean)
No. ADL Limitations[*]	0.82 (n = 738)	1.21 (n = 1281)
No. IADL Limitations[*]	0.95 (n = 738)	1.37 (n = 1281)

[*] $p < .001$

Receipt of Social Security

An issue that is of particular interest is whether the receipt of Social Security is related to whether a recipient is a citizen of the United States. A person only has to be a legal resident in the country to be able to acquire a Social Security number. For Puerto Ricans this is not an issue. Also, most Cuban Americans in this age cohort came to the United States as political refugees and thereby gained legal status. These two groups thus are different than the Mexican Americans in the sample, some of whom may have come to this country as undocumented workers. Some may have also come under the bracero[8] program and remained in the country to continue working here. Still others may be "native" citizens of the United States from the time the land that they lived on was annexed by the United States.

The survey did not ask about legal citizenship status. Because legal residence status is an issue for some Mexican Americans, these data were examined to see if a relation between receipt of Social Security and citizenship could be made. These data were analyzed to see if any conclusions could be reached about the unasked question of citizenship. For example, in all of the ethnic groups, proportionately more men receive Social Security than women. This may be explained by one of two possibilities. The first is that more men than women are legal residents or are citizens of the United States and hence are qualified to apply for the benefits. The second is that more men than women worked outside the home and were thus able to be eligible for the benefits. Neither together nor separately do these ideas support the proposition that receiving Social Security is correlated to citizenship. While the data are inconclusive regarding citizenship, interesting information is available about the respondents.

Of the 2019 recipients in this sample, only 1676 (83%) responded to the question, "Are you now receiving income from Social Security?" Of the 1676, 1322 (79 percent) said they receive Social Security benefits. As might be expected, those who receive Social Security immigrated at a significantly younger age (36.85 years) than the non-recipients (48.99 years) (p < .001).

Post Hospital Care

There were 479 (24 percent) of the 2001 respondents who had an overnight stay at the hospital in the last 12 months. The analysis examines the use of formal care (home health agency, nursing home, or a registered nurse) and informal care (family, spouse, friend, or neighbor) after hospitalization.

Table 4.12 reflects that family and spouse continue to be the greatest resource for the elders. However, it is surprising that only 25 elders were cared for by a friend or neighbor, slightly less than the number of elders cared for by a registered nurse (n = 26).[9]

The number cared for by a home health agency or a nursing home was very low (n = 2). In this analysis, it is not possible to explain the low rate of utilization of these resources. However, Estrada, Trevino, and Ray (1990)[10] state that for Mexican Americans several barriers to use of health services exist: "These barriers include but are not limited to language and cultural barriers, lack of transportation, geographic inaccessibility, financial constraints such as the cost of health care and limited health insurance coverage, and isolation from the mainstream culture" (p 27).

Table 4.12

Results of care provided post hospital by category

	Number	%[1]	%[2]
Cared for self	73	14.0	15.0
Cared for by family, spouse, friend, or neighbor	371	72.0	77.0
Cared for by a home health agency, nursing home or registered nurse	61	12.0	13.0
No care needed	12	2.0	3.0

[1] This percentage is based on the 517 total answers. Respondents were asked to answer all questions that applied to them.
[2] This percentage is based on the 479 respondents.

These studies support those of Cantor (1985) and Antonucci (1985),[11] showing that the spouse and the children are by far the most likely to provide care to an elder who has been hospitalized.

Another aspect of the analysis found that some elders receive assistance from the informal support system even though they also say that they provided care for themselves (SELFCARE variable). Twenty-two (30 percent) of the group who cared for themselves were also provided care by the informal support system. The chi-square showed that this relation was statistically significant at p < .01.

Additionally, of the 61 individuals who were cared for by the formal support system, 48 percent (29) were also provided care by the informal support system. This finding would indicate that use of formal support systems cannot be categorically interpreted as indicating that the family has abandoned the elder. However, due to the interdependence of the systems, it could indicate that the informal support system needs assistance in caring for some elders. Morris and Sherwood (1984)[12] state, "From this perspective, the formal members of the network can be seen as ancillary to the informal members" (p 82).

Education

According to Butler, Lewis and Sunderland (1991),[13] formal education greatly influences other socioeconomic areas of a person's life. In this study, having three years of formal education was the most frequent (497 times) response. Given that this cohort of respondents earned a living in an era when a high school education could be considered an adequate avenue to labor force participation, in this sample, only 38 (.02 percent) of the 2019 respondents had completed high school. As seen in Table 4.1 the mean number of formal years of education for the respondents is 6 years.

In further analysis of the educational level, the median years of education did not vary as widely as expected between males and females. The median years of education for males was 6.47 and for females it was 5.95. The analysis of variance results are statistically significant at p<.001.

Income

In order to give more significance to the findings of mean income, a high income category was developed that would allow further exploration of those who have earnings above the mean. The high income group was identified as those with incomes over $15,000 per year. Of the 1930 respondents who answered the income question, 193 or 10 percent, were in this category.

How income is distributed between Hispanic elderly men and women is important given that their labor force participation throughout their lifetime was also different. This sample revealed a statistically significant difference (p <.001) income for men and women. The men earn 16 percent more than women (see table 4.13).

Table 4.13

t-Test results on three variables by gender

	Men (Mean)	Women (Mean)	t Value	p Value
Income	$12,000	$10,050	-5.26	<.001
Education	6.7	5.9	-3.80	<.001
Total Community-Based Services Used	.8564	1.23	6.24	<.001

BIVARIATE RESULTS BY ETHNICITY

Further bivariate analyses were conducted to compare the findings for the total population to the findings for the three ethnic subgroups. The analysis of variance results on the total community-based services that are utilized by the three Hispanic elderly groups reflect a statistically significant difference (p < .001) in services used. When the comparison is being made among the three ethnic groups, on the average, the Mexican Americans are the lowest utilizers with a mean of .96 and the Puerto Ricans are highest with a mean of 1.48 (see table 4.14). Also, it is interesting to note that when analyzing service use by ethnic group and by gender, the range varies from a low of .78 by the Mexican American males to a high of 1.67 by the Puerto Rican females.

Another factor to consider is the average age of the frail population. The Puerto Rican group is the youngest, yet has a higher proportion of frail elders (see table 4.15). Again this fact could influence higher rates of utilization over their life span.

Table 4.14

Two-way analysis of variance results for
total community-based services utilized by ethnicity and gender

	Mexican Americans (Mean)	Cuban Americans (Mean)	Puerto Ricans (Mean)
Community-based services used*	0.96 (n = 937)	1.07 (n = 714)	1.48 (n = 368)
Community-based services used by males*	0.78 (n = 347)	0.84 (n = 268)	1.10 (n = 123)
Community-based services used by females*	1.06 (n = 590)	1.22 (n = 446)	1.67 (n = 245)

f = 24.384
*p < .001

Table 4.15

Two-way ANOVA results:
frailty by ethnicity and by age

	Mexican Americans (Mean)	Cuban Americans (Mean)	Puerto Ricans (Mean)
Age of frail[*]	76.25 (n = 255)	78.61 (n = 135)	75.53 (n = 127)
Age of non-frail[*]	72.41 (n = 682)	72.84 (n = 379)	71.59 (n = 241)
percent frail	27%	19%	35%

$f = 59.898$
[*] $p < .001$

State of residence may play an important role in the utilization of community-based services. Puerto Ricans are primarily located in New York and New Jersey. On the other hand, with 34 percent of its population being Mexican Americans, California has the largest number of Mexican Americans of all the states (GAO 1992).[14] These facts are particularly interesting since New York and California provide higher than average benefits to vulnerable populations (Topical Law Reports 1990).[15]

Mexican Americans are the lowest utilizers of community-based services whereas Puerto Ricans are the highest. The fact that Puerto Ricans are frail at a younger age may be a significant factor in their use of community-based services. In addition, the user of one service may be referred to other services; that is, once an elder enters the formal support system for one service s(he) is referred to others. This is particularly likely to be true in formal support systems that use case managers.

In conjunction with the use of community-based services, analyses of functional limitations by ethnicity were completed on this sample. Although the Cuban American elders are the oldest of the three populations, they have the fewest functional limitations (0.82). The average ADL limitation for all Hispanic elders is 1.07 (see table 4.16).

In comparing the three ethnic groups by total number of ADL limitations and level of frailty, there was no significant difference in the main effects of the analysis of variance among the three groups. A one-way analysis was performed on number of ADL limitations by ethnicity using the Scheffe test. The test is to see which groups are significantly different at the 0.05 level. These results reflected that Mexican Americans and Puerto Ricans are both different from the Cuban Americans. Also, the Puerto Ricans are different from both of the other groups.

Table 4.16

Two-way analysis of variance results
of functional limitations (TOTADL) by
ethnicity and by frailty

	Mexican Americans (Mean)	Cuban Americans (Mean)	Puerto Ricans (Mean)
Total ADLs*	1.12 (n = 937)	0.82 (n = 714)	1.39 (n = 368)
Total ADLs and frail	3.53 (n = 255)	3.67 (n = 135)	3.58 (n = 127)
Total ADLs and not frail	0.23 (n = 682)	0.15 (n = 579)	0.24 (n = 241)

*$p < .001$

The next analysis by ethnicity was completed on the cognitive limitations (IADLS) that the elders identified. The findings were consistent in that the Cuban Americans, although the oldest, experience the least number of cognitive limitations (0.98) of the three Hispanic groups. Here the mean number of IADL limitations for the total sample is 1.22. The Puerto Rican elders are the group with the most cognitive limitations (1.41) on average (see table 4.17).

Table 4.17

Two-way analysis of variance results
of cognitive limitations (TOTIADL) by
ethnicity and by frailty

	Mexican Americans (Mean)	Cuban (Mean)	Puerto Rican (Mean)
Total IADLs[**]	1.32 (n = 937)	0.98 (n = 714)	1.41 (n = 368)
Total IADLs and frail[*]	3.34 (n = 255)	3.27 (n = 135)	3.13 (n = 127)
Total IADLs and not frail[*]	0.57 (n = 682)	0.45 (n = 579)	0.50 (n = 241)

[*] $p < .10$
[**] $p < .001$

The same Scheffe test was used to analyze the differences among the means for IADL limitations of the groups. In this analysis, the Mexican American and Puerto Rican elders were different from the Cuban elders at the 0.05 level.

In looking at both functional and cognitive limitations, it is interesting that Cuban Americans have the lowest number of limitations, yet use services at the same rate as Mexican Americans. Mexican Americans use the fewest services of all the groups. This finding supports Markides et al. (1983)[16] who found that older Mexican Americans were more isolated from others to an extent beyond what much of the literature seems to suggest. They also found that the Chicano elders were isolated from relatives and an even larger proportion was isolated from non-relatives.

It is also interesting that of all three ethnic groups, Cubans are the least likely to speak English. From these data one can infer that fewer than two functional or cognitive limitations and an inability to speak English are not necessarily barriers to accessing community-based services (see table 4.18).

Table 4.18

Analysis of variance results: services used by those who speak English and those who speak Spanish

Number of Services Used by	Speak English (Mean)	Speak Spanish (Mean)	Sig. p
Mexican Americans	0.94	0.98	.55
Cuban Americans	0.85	1.20	.001
Puerto Ricans	1.33	1.64	.001

Interestingly, of the three groups, a higher proportion of Mexican Americans, 680 (84 percent) receive Social Security. Next are Puerto Ricans who report that 212 or 79 percent receive Social Security. Only 430 or 71 percent of Cuban American elders report themselves as being recipients of Social Security benefits. As noted earlier, since the three groups had different immigration patterns one would expect the rates of receipt of Social Security to be different. However, since the question of legal status is most applicable to Mexican Americans, the results are unexpected.

The respondents (n = 1,185) immigrated at a mean age of 40 years. The age at which the three ethnic groups immigrated was significantly different (p < .001). The Mexican Americans immigrated at the youngest age (27 years) and the Cuban Americans at the oldest age (50 years). The Puerto Ricans immigrated at an average age of 35 years.

It is logical to expect that age of immigration influences an individual's potential earnings and, consequently, Social Security earnings. That is, the younger a person is at immigration, the more likely (s)he is to acquire skills to earn higher levels of income throughout the years of labor force participation. Also, a younger immigrant would work over a longer period of time and earn more quarterly credits for Social Security benefits.

And, in fact, in looking at the immigration and the Social Security data together, this theory holds. The Cubans immigrated at a later age and represent the fewest recipients of Social Security. However, in considering annual income data, the theory does not hold. As elders the Cubans have the highest income level although they are the oldest at time of immigration. Income from sources other than Social Security may account for the higher income levels of Cuban Americans.

Years of formal education vary considerably by ethnicity and by gender (see table 4.19). Interestingly, the male Mexican American elders have fewer years of formal education than the Puerto Rican males, yet the income of Mexican American males is significantly higher than that of the Puerto Rican males. Among females, Cuban Americans have a significantly higher level of education.

Interestingly, the Cuban elders' mean level of education is higher ($p<.001$) than the other two groups, which probably influenced their higher income, but the Puerto Ricans and the Mexican Americans have exactly the same mean education level although Mexican Americans' income level is significantly higher than that of Puerto Ricans. The reason for this disparity is not clear from the research. It may be possible that this is due to the higher levels of frailty that are experienced by Puerto Ricans.

Cuban American men and women and Puerto Rican men have higher levels of education. Mexican American men and women and Puerto Rican females have fewer years of education than the mean for all elders. There is a possibility that differences among the three ethnic groups in levels of education are due to social class. However, these data do not permit such conclusions.

As seen in Table 4.19 Cuban Americans have the highest income per year and the difference among the three groups is statistically significant, $p < .01$.

Table 4.19

Means and analysis of variance results of key
variables by ethnicity and gender

	Mexican Americans (Mean)	Cuban Americans (Mean)	Puerto Ricans (Mean)	F Stat	Sig. of F
Income	$10,650	$11,950	$9,649	14.611	<.001
Male Income	$11,500	$13,500	$10,150	19.672	<.001
Female Income	$10,050	$10,900	$9,000		<.001
Education Level	5.21	8.11	5.23	81.187	<.001
Male Education Level	5.49	8.80	5.82	15.628	<.001
Female Education Level	5.08	7.69	4.92		<.001

The mean income earned by the three groups taken together is
$10,850. The income variable was used as a continuous and dichotomous
variable with high or low income. The results are consistent even when
the income is recoded to indicate high income. Again, Cuban elders are
more likely to be in the high income category. Sadly, only six percent
(n = 21) of Puerto Rican elders have annual incomes of over $15,000 per
year.

All three groups of men earned more money than the three groups of women. However, Puerto Rican men earn the least of the three male groups. Mexican American women earn the exact mean for the females in the total sample–less than their Cuban but more than their Puerto Rican counterparts. However, the difference is not statistically significant. Cuban American men and women as well as Mexican American males have more than the mean income for all elders in the sample ($10,850). The other three groups, Puerto Rican men and women and Mexican American females earn less than the average. In summary, among the three groups, the Puerto Ricans are the poorest and the Puerto Rican females are the poorest of the poor.

The last area that was analyzed for the three ethnic groups was the area of post hospital care. Individuals who cared for themselves when released from the hospital were analyzed by ethnicity. While not statistically significant, Mexican Americans were the least likely to say they provided care for themselves (three percent) and Puerto Ricans were the most likely (five percent) to be in this situation (see table 4.20).

Another interesting finding is that when post hospital formal system care is analyzed by ethnicity, the Puerto Ricans again show up as most likely to use the formal system. Further analyses were done to identify possible differences among the three ethnic groups and their informal support systems. Three hundred seventy-one elders were provided post hospital care by their informal support systems. Of the three groups, the Puerto Ricans were most likely and Mexican Americans elders least likely to be provided care by their informal support system. However, the difference was not statistically significant.

Table 4.20

Chi-square results among Hispanic elders
and post hospital care

	Mexican Americans (Mean)	Cuban Americans (Mean)	Puerto Ricans (Mean)
Hospitalization Overnight*	21.8 (n = 204)	23.0 (n = 164)	30.2 (n = 111)
Informal Care Post Hospital (n = 371)	17.2 (n = 161)	18.3 (n = 131)	21.5 (n = 79)
Formal Care Post Hospital** (n = 61)	2.0 (n = 19)	2.5 (n = 18)	6.5 (n = 24)
Cared for Self (n = 73)	2.8 (n = 26)	4.1 (n = 29)	4.9 (n = 18)

$x^2 = 19.156$
*$p < .01$
**$p < .0001$

SUMMARY

The bivariate results confirm differences among the three Hispanic groups. Furthermore, the findings support the theory that more differences exist than similarities in areas of health, education, and income. These are also significant differences in number of community-based services used by ethnicity. Additionally, the age at which the elders are frail is different. There is a strong relation between being frail and using more than five community-based services. If these relations are significant in the ordinary least squares analyses, the hypothesis concerning frailty and use of services will be supported.

Mini Analysis

The total community-based services that were used in the survey were counted and used as an internal variable ranging from 1 to 10. However, additional bivariate analyses were also completed on each individual community service to determine use of each service by different predictive variables. The following predictive variables that were thus analyzed follow with the analytic results.

1. *Being Frail*–Frailty is positively related to use of all the services except senior meals and senior centers. The likely explanation is that mobility is a frequently identified limitation and both of these activities require that a person be mobile in order to leave the house.

2. *Speaking English*–Being able to speak English is associated with the use of senior centers, senior meals, visiting nurses and home health services. This finding may be more telling than is obvious at first glance. It is very likely that speaking English enables Hispanic elders to enjoy activities which require some socialization. The latter two services may require an ability to speak English to be able to maneuver one's way through the bureaucracies that provide assistance in the home.

3. *Income*–The t-test results showed no relation between income and use of any of the ten services.

4. *Years of Education*–Years of education was a factor in use of all services except use of senior transportation, senior centers, and senior meals.

5. *Gender*–There was no association between gender and the use of senior centers, senior meals, telephone checks, and senior church programs.

6. *Self-Perceived Health Status*–There was no association between self-perceived health status and using senior centers, telephone checks, or church senior programs.

Another phase of the mini analysis was to look at services used by the three groups. As can be seen in table 4.21, the Puerto Ricans who are the most frail use higher levels of services that come into the house, i.e., homemaker services, visiting nurse and home health services. An interesting finding is that of the three groups, Cuban Americans proportionally use the most food stamps and Mexican Americans use the most Meals on Wheels. However, the differences in how the three groups use home health services is not significant.

Table 4.21

Chi-square results of use of community-based
services by the three ethnic groups

Service	Mexican Americans	Cuban Americans	Puerto Ricans
Senior transportation*	9.4%	18.16%	22.6%
Senior center*	12.9%	9.4%	19.9%
Meals on wheels	*9.1%	3.4%	3.5%
Senior meals**	15.5%	10.2%	15.8%
Homemaker service*	6.6%	4.8%	16.0%
Phone checks	4.4%	3.5%	4.1%
Visiting nurse*	9.1%	9.5%	17.9%
Home health Service	4.2%	5.8%	6.8%
Food stamps*	16.2%	40.3%	36.1%
Senior church program*	8.6%	2.7%	5.5%

*p < .00001
**p < .001

Additionally, several predictor variables were used in Scheffe procedures. This was done to find out which of the ethnic groups are significantly different from each other at the 0.05 level. These results add another dimension of analyses to that provided by analysis of variance results.

1.   In the use of Medicaid, Mexican Americans are least likely to be covered by the program.

2.   In looking at number of children, age, and post hospital informal support by the three ethnic groups, no two groups were significantly different from each other.

3.   Income level was higher for Mexican Americans and Cuban Americans than for Puerto Ricans. It was also higher for the Cuban Americans than for the two other groups. All three groups were significantly different ($p < .001$).

4.   In the areas of being frail, speaking English and total ADL limitations, the Mexican American and Puerto Rican elders were different from the Cuban Americans. Also, the Puerto Ricans were significantly different from the other elders, but Cubans and Mexicans were not different from each other despite education, income, and age differences.

5.   The Puerto Rican elders use more services than the Mexican Americans and the Cuban Americans but Cubans and Mexicans were not different from each other despite education, income, and age differences. The results of the Sheffe test are at variance with the analysis of variance results.

6.   Fewer Cuban Americans elders speak Spanish compared to the two other groups.

7.   With respect to age of immigration and the receipt of Social Security, the Mexican Americans immigrated at a much younger age than either of the other two groups, while the Cuban Americans immigrated at a significantly older age.

8.   Of the three groups, Puerto Ricans are most likely to
      live alone.

In summary, this mini analysis provided some insights into what services are used by people with certain characteristics and also services that are used in different proportions by the three ethnic groups. The next chapter answers the research questions via multivariate analysis.

Notes

[1] Frances Carp, *Factors in Utilization of Services by the Mexican-American Elderly* (1968 Palo Alto, CA: American Institutes for Research), 4.

[2] Marin and Marin, 6.

[3] Nursing homes use level frailty as the determinate for admission. However, as seen in Appendix A, different states use different or varied criteria to base the eligibility.

[4] Another important category that has been discussed by previous researchers is age. Crouch (1972) found that Mexican Americans considered old age to start between 50-55 years.

[5] M.E. Jackson , 1991, looked at the different combinations of ADLs and IADLs that states used to define frailty.

[6] *Report of the Commonwealth Fund Commission on Elderly People Living Alone,* Chapter 5.

[7] Lacayo, Chapter 2 and Martin and Martin, Chapter 1.

[8] A Mexican farm laborer brought into the United States temporarily for migrant work in harvesting crops, (Webster's New World Dictionary, p. 171).

[9] It is possible that the registered nurses came from home health agencies. If so, the numbers would change dramatically for use of home health agencies.

[10] The authors Antonio L. Estrada, Fernando M. Trevino and Laura A. Ray, 1990, analyze the underutilization of home health agencies and nursing homes by elderly Hispanics.

[11] Toni C. Antonucci, *Personal Characteristics, Social Support, and Social Behavior* (1985; New York: Van Nostrand Reinhold Company) 94-128. Marjorie Cantor and Virginia Little, Aging and Social Care (1985; New York: Van Nostrand Reinhold Company) 745-781.

[12] John N. Morris and Sylvia Sherwood, 1984, research the interdependence of the informal and the formal support systems.

[13] Robert N. Butler, Myrna Lewis and Trey Sunderland, 1991, suggest a relationship between formal education and subsequent socioeconomic status.

[14] US General Accounting Office, 1-26.

[15] Topical Law Reports, 1990.

[16] Markides, 115-138.

V

Multiple Regression Results

INTRODUCTION

The essence of the study was to look at community-based services utilization within the context of frailty, English speaking language skills, geographical distance between elders and children, size of the informal support system, gender, and ethnicity. In order to answer the research questions, multiple regression was used to determine the influence of each variable on the use of community-based services as well as the interrelationship between the dependent and the explanatory variables.

This chapter reports the results by hypotheses. The results have been grouped into two parts. The first two hypotheses report the findings for those research questions that look only at Mexican American elders. The last four report the results that compare the three ethnic populations.

SUBSAMPLE SELECTION

The dependent variable, total community-based service used (TOTCBS) was reconstructed for use in the multivariate analysis. A 33 percent sample of the non-users was randomly selected to remain in the sample for the multivariate analysis. The recoding and restructuring made the distribution of the dependent variable more nearly normal. Additionally, this procedure did not compromise the integrity of the distribution since non-users were randomly selected. In addition to this subsample selection, the total number of community-based services used were recoded and assigned to the following values:

1 = 0 services used

2 = 1 service used

3 = 2 services used

4 = 3 or 4 services used

5 = 5 to 10 services used

In this analysis the full statistical model is:

TOTCBS = b_0 + b_1 (WTHSSUP) + b_2 (FRAIL)+ b_3 (TOTADL + b_4 (TOTIADL) + b_5 (POORHLTH) + b_6(INCOME) + b_7 (SPEAK) + b_8 (AGE) + b_9 (PRICAN) +b_{10} (MEXAM) + b_{11} (EDUC) + b_{12} +(GENDER) + b_{13} (TIME) + b_{14} (MCAID) + b_{15} (HOSP) + b_{16} (INFRMSS) + (INTERCEPT)

The total sample for the multivariate analysis is 1,412. The sample included a total Mexican American sample of 614. The Cuban American sample is 504, and the Puerto Rican sample size is 281. The reference group in the regression is the Cuban Americans because they have the highest income.

In the full statistical model there was a multicollinearity problem between frail and having ADL limitations and/or IADL limitations. Other models were tested using the variables total ADL limitations and total IADL limitations without the variable testing for frailty. In these models there was also multicollinearity between total ADL limitations and total IADL limitations. In other models that included level of frailty and total ADL limitations or level of frailty and total IADL limitations, multicollinearity was again found among all three variables.

As a result, the model that was finally used dropped both total ADL limitations and total IADL limitations. This was done without having to create an interaction term because the variable frail is constructed from the total ADL limitations and IADL limitations.

In this first analysis, regression analysis is used to test how well the independent variables predict the use of community-based services that are utilized by the Mexican American sample population.

Hypothesis: Those Mexican American elders who utilize the greatest number of formal services will also be the elders who are frail.

This hypothesis looked at the 255 frail Mexican Americans and their use of services. The assumption was that these frail elders would use a greater number of services than the non-frail Mexican American elders.

The bivariate analysis supported the hypothesis. Frail Mexican American elders who use services use 1.61 services compared to the non-frail who use 0.92 service.

Although the findings at the bivariate level support the theory, it was also expected that the sample of frail elders would use even higher levels of community-based services since socioeconomic data for these elders revealed high levels of poverty and poor health. Initially, the multivariate analysis did not support the hypothesis. In order to further test the model, interaction terms were constructed by using the variables for being Mexican American and age of respondents. The variables being frail and age of respondents were used with Mexican Americans because these two variables were consistently significant as indicators of frailty. These terms were then included in the model.

However, because Mexican American elders was a constant, the interaction terms could not be used as developed. Finally, the following model which included only the Mexican Americans was used:

$$TOTCBS = b_0 + b_1 (GENDER) + b_2 (SPEAK) + b_3 (INCOME) + b_4 (EDUC) + b_5 (AGE) + b_6 (FRAIL) + b_7 (WTHSSUP) + b_8 (POORHLTH) + b_9 (MCAID) + b_{10} (HOSP) + b_{11} (NUMBER\ OF\ CHDN) + b_{12} (INFORMAL\ POST\ HOSP\ CARE) + b_{13} (TIME) + b_{14} (INTERCEPT)$$

Table 5.1 presents the results of the multivariate analysis for this model. The variables that are significant in the model are having been in the hospital in the last year, level of income, having self-reported poor health status, and living with someone.

The interesting finding is that two of the most significant variables, living with someone and income, show a negative relation with the total community-based services used. Throughout the analyses, having higher levels of income and living with someone else result in lower use of services. The two variables, having been in the hospital and self reporting to be in poor health are variables that are significant in a positive direction. The other variables in the model were not significant; the adjusted R square is .13.

The hypothesis of frailty being related to use of community-based services was not supported by the multivariate analysis. However, self-identified poor health and having been hospitalized within the last year are predictors of use of services. These last two variables are more significant than the definition of frailty in predicting use of services when Mexican American elders are frail.

Identical data analyses were done on Cuban American and Puerto Rican elders (see tables 5.2 and 5.3). As can be seen, it is the frail Puerto Rican elders who are more likely to use community-based services.

In looking at the Cuban Americans, the results were significantly different from the Mexican Americans (see table 5.2). Being on Medicaid was the predictor variable with the strongest relation to use of community-based services. Given that Cuban Americans also have the highest income, this was unexpected. To explore this interesting finding at the bivariate level, crosstab analyses were run on Cuban Americans who had high versus low income. There are a total of 193 elderly Hispanics who have high income. Of these, 50 percent (96) are Cuban Americans. However, the Cuban Americans with high income account for only 13 percent of the total Cuban population. Therefore, Cuban Americans also are represented in very poor economic circumstances. Hence, they qualify for Medicaid.

The next significant predictor variables are the income and age of Cuban American respondents. As previously discussed, their mean age is the highest of the three groups. They are the oldest but the least frail. In respect to income, the finding is consistent with the two other groups, i.e., as income increases use of community-based services decreases.

The last three significant variables are time it takes the child to reach the parent's home, being frail, and having been hospitalized in the last 12 months. Given that the time variable was not significant with Mexican Americans who have more children, it was surprising that it was significant with this particular group. On the other hand the other two variables were expected to be significant.

Variables that had been expected to be significant in this analysis and were not include ability to speak English and being in poor health.

Table 5.1

Results of multiple regression analysis
for frail Mexican Americans' use of services

Variable	Estimated Coefficient	Beta	Sig. t
TIME	-.012449	-.011990	.8190
GENDER	-.073017	-.031382	.5468
POORHLTH	.314607	.092927	.0892*
MCAID	.122896	.053586	3136
SPEAK	.028371	.012645	.8032
INFORM SUP SYS	-.044753	-.015834	.8649
NO. OF CHDN	.007342	.020546	.6932
EDUC	-.004365	-.014891	.7862
AGE	.014019	.086649	.1085
LIVE W/SOMEONE	-.448010	-.181408	.0013***
INCOME	-.106776	-.112862	.0481
FRAIL	.131997	.053663	.3521
HOSP	.520076	.202957	.0301*
(CONSTANT)	1.591436	.0209	

Multiple R .39867
R Square .15894
Adjusted R^2 .12678
F = 4.94249
Signif. F = .0001
*$p < .10$
**$p < .05$
***$p < .001$

Table 5.2

Results of multiple regression analysis
for frail Cuban Americans' use of services

Variable	Estimated Coefficient	Beta	Sig. t
TIME	.108282	.108136	.0529**
INFORM SUP SYS	-.406582	-.150880	.1877
GENDER	.029290	.012687	.8203
SPEAK	-.037915	-.016375	.7913
MCAID	.510381	.232563	.0002****
AGE	.025556	.165229	.0047***
POORHLTH	.030015	.007920	.8921
CHDN	.015467	.02303	.6677
INCOME	-.144692	-.178046	.0032***
EDUC	-.002312	-.009527	.8758
LIVE WITH SOMEONE	-.211515	-.083719	.1567
FRAIL	.288664	.109672	.0810*
HOSPITAL OVERNIGHT	.562881	.223966	.0475**
(CONSTANT)	.439197		.5170

Multiple R .51660
R Square .26687
Adjusted R^2 .23077
F = 7.39247
Signif. F = .0001
*p < .10
**p < .05
***p < .01
****p < .001

Table 5.3

Results of multiple regression analysis
for frail Puerto Ricans'
use of services

Variable	Estimated Coefficient	Beta	Sig. t
TIME	-.151142	-.136699	.0733[*]
INFORM SUP SYS	-.534939	-.173629	.1252
GENDER	-.109405	-.041400	.5807
SPEAK	.060123	.024521	.7581
MCAID	.093503	.037443	.6264
AGE	.022544	.124358	.1038
POORHLTH	-.010789	-.003103	.9676
CHDN	.001217	.002938	.9688
INCOME	-.217682	-.171314	.0401[**]
EDUC	-.024624	-.063390	.4363
LIVE WITH SOMEONE	-.487420	-.197211	.0174[**]
FRAIL	.512752	.202315	.0149[**]
HOSPITALIZATION OVERNIGHT	.715198	.266280	.0202[**]
(CONSTANT)	1.585569		.1530

Multiple R .52455
R Square .27515
Adjusted R^2 .21016
F = 4.23396
Signif. F = .0001
[*]p < .10
[**]p < .05

The Puerto Ricans were also examined for use of community-based services using the same model. It was interesting that unlike the Cuban Americans, there were five significant variables in the model. However, even though Puerto Ricans are the poorest of the three groups and would most likely be receiving Medicaid, that variable was not significant. Being frail, living with someone, having been hospitalized in the last year, income, and time it takes for the child to reach their parent's home were the significant predictor variables.

It is surprising that, like the Cuban Americans, the Puerto Ricans with higher incomes tend to use fewer services. As a group they are poorer, and use more services than the other two groups. Yet this group is like the other two in that they use fewer services as income rises. Research has not delved into the use of paid assistance by the higher income groups within these ethnic groups. The adjusted R square for the Mexican Americans is the lowest of the three groups indicating the least predictive value of the expected variables. This indicates a need for more research with this population.

> Hypothesis: The more children who live within one hour
> from the Mexican American elder, the less likely the
> elder will utilize community-based services.

Of the 937 Mexican Americans respondents who were included in the analysis of this hypothesis, 97 percent (353) of the elders live 30 minutes or less from their children. As a matter of fact, 64 percent live within 10 minutes from their children. Yet, in analyzing the distance from their children and the role it may play in the elders' use of community-based services, there was no significant relation. Interestingly, although Mexican Americans have more children per respondent that the other two groups, the time predictor variable was not significant for that group. Another interesting result was the fact that for Puerto Ricans, the time variable had a negative relation with use of community-based services. So the closer the children are, the more services Puerto Ricans use. The findings did not support the hypothesis for Mexican Americans. Neither do the data support the assumption that the time it takes children to get to the Mexican American parents home is a significant determinant of total community-based services utilized.

Another analysis was done by restructuring the time variable. The time it takes to get to the Mexican American elders' home was divided into less than 30 minutes or more than 30 minutes in order to reanalyze the data. In spite of the restructuring of the time variable, there is no significant difference in community-based service utilization between those who live within 30 minutes from their children and those who live further away. The closer group of respondents use 1.91 services and the group that is further away uses 1.7 services. The mean for the total sample population is 1.8.

The bivariate analyses also supported the finding that the time it takes a child to get to his/her parents' home is not a significant variable in relation to use of community-based services.

The multivariate analysis supported the results from the ANOVA which had not shown any relation among the time it takes for a child to get to the elders' home, total community-based services used, and being Mexican American (see table 5.1). These results may be inconclusive given that the question asked was, "How quickly can any one of your children get to your home?" The answers did not provide the variance that is required for the analysis.

> Hypothesis: Verbal English language skills are positively
> related to utilization of community-based services.

In looking at the total community-based services that are utilized by all the elders who speak English the hypothesis was not supported. In all three groups, elders who spoke English utilized fewer community-based services than those who spoke no English, but the difference between the ones who spoke English and those who do not is not significant for Mexican American elders while the difference for the Cuban American and Puerto Rican elders is significant at $p < .001$. Other factors besides being able to communicate in English seem to be important in accessing community-based services (see tables 5.5 and 5.6).

Of special note is the fact that among the three non-English speaking groups, Mexican American elders who do not speak English use the fewest services. Conversely, non-English speaking Puerto Ricans use the most.

In looking at elders who do speak English and their use of services, again, Mexican Americans use the fewest services. Among all the elders who speak English and those who do not, Puerto Ricans consistently use the greatest number of community-based services. However, of the three groups, the elderly Mexican Americans exhibit the most consistency in the utilization of services (means = 0.96 percent and 0.94 percent) regardless of language proficiency.

Table 5.4

Multiple regression results estimating total community based services used by those who speak English

Variable	Estimated Coefficient	Beta	Sig. t
EDUC	-.006829	-.025125	.4644
AGE	.021218	.129538	.0001***
MEXAM	.030849	-.013300	.7133
GENDER	-.040115	.016693	.5956
SPEAK ENGLISH	.61490E-04	2.854E-04	.9929
POOR HEALTH	.093501	.026519	.4184
INCOME	-.136611	-.145173	.0001****
LIVE WITH SOMEONE	-.360590	-.144915	.0001****
FRAIL	.273471	.107858	.0022***
PUERTO RICAN	.119417	.04077	.2465
INFORM SUP SYS	-.265452	-.093059	.0975*
NO. OF CHDN	-.004378	-.011373	.7254
MCAID	.261616	.115539	.0006***
HOSP	.615751	.237927	.0001***
(CONSTANT)	1.124054		.0064

Multiple R .45498
R Square .20700
Adj. R Square .19427
Signif F = .000
F = 16.25913
*p < .10
**.005
***p < .001
****p < .0001

The multivariate analysis also disproved the hypothesis in that the ability to speak English was not significant in the use of community-based services. As can be seen in table 5.4, the regression coefficient reflects that if a person speaks English, (s)he will only increase his/her use of community-based services by .61490E-04.

Table 5.5

Chi-Square results
for speaking
English by ethnicity

	Mexican Americans	Cuban American	Puerto Ricans
Speak English*	(n = 267) 28.5%	(n = 156) 21.8%*	(n = 143) 38.9%*
Speak Spanish	(n = 670) 71.5%	(n = 558) 78.2%	(n = 225) 61.1%

*p < .0001

Table 5.6

Two-way analysis of variance
results of total community
based services used by ethnicity
and speaking English

	Mexican Americans (Mean)	Cuban (Mean)	Puerto Rican (Mean)
Community-Based Services Used[*]	0.96 (n = 937)	1.07 (n = 714)	1.48 (n = 368)
Community-Based Services Used and Speak English[*]	0.94 (n = 267)	0.74 (n = 156)	1.28 (n = 143)
Community-Based Services Used and Speak Spanish[*]	0.96 (n = 670)	1.16 (n = 558)	1.61 (n = 225)

[*]p < .005

Hypothesis: The size of the respondents' informal support
network has a significant predictive power for Hispanic
elders to remain in the community even when health and
financial status are controlled.

This analysis required a statistical model which included other variables found in the dataset that identified the informal support system. Therefore, two models which used Cuban Americans as the reference group were constructed. They are:

TOTCBS = b_0 + b_1 (AGE) + b_2 (MEXAM) + b_3 (INFRMSS)+ b_4 (INCOME) + b_5 (SPEAK) + b_6 (POORHLTH)+ b_7 (GENDER) + b_8 (CHDN) + b_9 (WTHSSUP)+ b_{10} (EDUC) + b_{11} + (FRAIL) + b_{12} (PRICAN)+ b_{13} INTERCEPT)

TOTCBS =b_0+ b_1 (PRICAN)+ b_2 (INFRMSS + b_3 (CHDN) +b_4 (INCOME) + b_5 (POORHLTH) + b_6 (WTHSSUP) +b_7 (FRAIL) + b_8 (MEXAM) + b_9 (SPEAK) + b_{10} (INTERCEPT)

The two models were constructed in order to explore the results of both a reduced model and a full model. The full model would be expected to have a higher adjusted R square due to taking into account more variation. Significant differences in the effects that were found in the two models are reported.

In comparing the full model (table 5.7) to the reduced model (table 5.8), the full model had an adjusted R square of .18 and the reduced model had an adjusted R square of .16. Interestingly, the four explanatory variables that were significant in both models, were very similar in their effect on the dependent variable. In the full model, being frail is slightly less significant.

The reduced model only included the explanatory variables that tested the hypothesis. The full model was constructed to include the variables in the basic model as well as the two variables that identified the informal support system and number of children that the respondent had.

Table 5.7

Results of multiple regression analysis
for informal support system as
predictor of use of services-full model

VARIABLE	B	BETA	Sig. t
PRICAN	.121787	.041280	.2402
HOSP	.425153	.164280	.0001**
GENDER	-.048831	-.020320	.5208
NO OF CHDN	-.002710	-.007038	.8290
AGE	.024286	.148268	.0001**
POOR HEALTH	.088242	.025028	.4482
SPEAK ENGLISH	-.024571	-.010603	.7425
INCOME	-.154960	-.164673	.0001**
EDUC	-.011552	-.042504	.2147
LIVE WITH SOMEONE	-.401274	-.161265	.0001**
FRAIL	.280424	.110592	.0018*
MEXAM	-.083074	-.035646	.3170
(CONSTANT)	1.138421		.0061

Multiple R .43955
R Square .19320
Adjusted R^2 .18213
F = 17.44153
Signif. F = .000
*p < .001
**p < .0001

These data provide an excellent opportunity to examine the role of the family informal support network on the use of community-based services. In both models, the inclusion of these independent variables which measure the informal support system (number of children, live with someone) serves to test the strength of the informal support system while controlling for health and financial status. The models include the variables being frail, self reporting poor health, and having been in the hospital during the previous year as the health indicators. The income variable, being Mexican American, being Puerto Rican, speaking English, gender, years of education and age of respondent are the important socio-demographic indicators.

In both the full (see table 5.7) and reduced (see table 5.8) models, the variable having been hospitalized in the previous year was initially dropped due to a problem with multicollinearity. The variable had been included because of its importance as an indicator of overall health status. However, there was multicollinearity between having been hospitalized and having an informal support system which means the respondent was cared for by a spouse, child, friend, or neighbor after being hospitalized. When the regression was run with the informal support system, the full model resulted in an adjusted R square of .16710 and the reduced model had one of .14692. Subsequently, having been hospitalized was substituted for having an informal support system post hospitalization. As can be seen in tables 5.7 and 5.8, both models are better predictors of use of community-based services with the independent variable of being hospitalized.

If Hispanic elders live with someone, they will use few community-based services regardless of health issues. The fact that living with someone plays a role in the non-use of community-based services is expected. However, the fact that having children is not significant in the use of services is not expected since the literature reports that spouses and children are the main source of care for elders. The finding that a high income level indicates lower use of community-based services is expected. As a whole, these findings are consistent with previous findings.

Table 5.8

Results of multiple regression analysis
with total community-based services
dependent variable-reduced model

Variable	Estimated Coefficient	BETA	Sig. t
FRAIL	.398430	.157131	.0001[*]
LIVE WITH SOMEONE	-.424440	-.170575	.0001[*]
MEXAM	-.062070	-.026761	.4452
SPEAK ENGLISH	-.087781	-.037878	.2287
HOSP	.427420	.165156	.0001[*]
NO OF CHDN	-.004826	-.012535	.7011
INCOME	-.170470	-.181154	.0001[*]
POOR HEALTH	.069466	.019702	.5542
PRICAN	.115009	.038982	.2600
(CONSTANT)	2.895873		.0001

Multiple R .41355
R Square .17102
Adjusted R^2 .16251
F = 20.10319
Signif. F = .000
[*] p < .001

For example, some studies suggest that having an informal support system may be the most important factor in caring for elders who are in the community. Also, Hispanic elders have a tendency to not use the formal support system and, if they have higher incomes, the reluctance to go outside the family for assistance may become accentuated. Some studies also found that having female children, and in particular one female child who will provide necessary care, is more significant in caring for elders in the community than number of children that are in the informal support system. This study only looked at having children as a factor in the use of community-based services and did not look at gender of the children.

In both models, the importance of having an informal support system, i.e., living with someone, is very significant as a predictor of use of services. It is important to note that having children, however, is not a significant predictor variable. Additionally, the variable of self-perceived poor health is not an important indicator of using community-based services. However, being frail has a significant relation with use of services.

Given the earlier discussion that half as many Hispanic elders see themselves being in poor health as are categorized as being frail, it appears that the elders have correctly labeled themselves. This conclusion builds on the previous finding that frail elders do use more services. Nevertheless, the hypothesis was not fully supported since ability to remain in the community could not be measured with the data.

> Hypothesis: Ethnicity is a predictor of rates of service
> utilization among Mexican American, Cuban American,
> and Puerto Ricans.

The preliminary results from the ANOVA revealed a total mean of 1.09 of community-based services used for all three groups of Hispanic elders. The data reveal that elderly Mexican Americans use the least number of services with a mean of .96. The Cuban Americans used the next number of services with a mean of 1.07, and Puerto Ricans used the most with a mean of 1.48. The variation between groups was significant (.001); however, post hoc Scheffe tests reveal that the Puerto Ricans differ from Cubans and Mexican Americans but these latter two groups are not significantly different from each other.

The multivariate analysis, however, did not support the hypothesis as neither being Mexican American nor Puerto Rican was significant in the use of community-based services once the ethnic groups were taken into account (see table 5.4 on page 90). The differences of use of services by ethnicity may be masked by the stronger significance of age, income, living with someone, being frail, receiving Medicaid, and having been hospitalized.

Hypothesis: There will be differences in the sample
population based on gender. These differences will be in
the areas of income, education, and number of formal
services utilized.

This relationship of the variables was first tested with bivariate
statistics using t-tests. The results supported the hypothesis at the .0001
level (see table 5.9). The mean income level for men was significantly
different from that of women as were level of education and use of
services. Men had higher incomes, level of education, and used fewer
services.

Table 5.9

Student's t-Test results:
gender differences in income, education
and utilization rates

Variables	t-Value	p Value
Income	-5.26	.000
Education	-3.80	.000
Community-Based Services Used	6.24	.000

Next, ordinary least squares regression was used to perform the
estimation of the multivariate analysis (see table 5.4).

The adjusted R square was .16. In this model, income was the only
variable that was significant. For each increase of $4,999 in income a
person used -.16 less services. Thus, once income was controlled, there
were no gender differences found.

SUMMARY

The findings from the multivariate analysis did support some of the hypotheses. Use of community-based services by Hispanic elders is influenced by being frail, age, and having been hospitalized. Having children in close proximity is not a significant factor in the use of services and neither is the ability to speak English. In addition, those with higher income, use fewer services on average, and respondents who live with others tend to use fewer services.

The multivariate analysis did support the theory that differences exist among Mexican Americans, Cuban Americans, or Puerto Ricans in their use of services when the analysis is performed on each group. However, when the analysis is completed with the ethnicity variable, the differences disappear. For the total sample, health, income, and support factors account for more of the explanatory variance than ethnicity.

The results on income and its impact on use of services are interesting in that the more income an elder has, the less likely (s)he is to use community-based services. Yet, the bivariate analyses confirmed that Cuban Americans have the highest income of the three ethnic groups, but not the lowest utilization of services. This suggests that income is an important factor in the prediction of services although not the only important factor. However, income may be an important a factor in predicting use of services as is the ethnicity variable. Within each ethnic group, income works in the direction found, i.e., inverse to use of services. This supports findings by Markides (1983) that being Mexican American was not a factor in use of services.

The results of the regression depicted a community-based elderly population that is assisted by its informal support network. The negative relation between the variables total community-based services used and living with someone supported the assumption that there is a significant relation between the informal support network and the elders' use or non-use of community-based services. Another strong relation was between the informal support system (INFRMSS) variable and the use of community-based services. The informal support system variable was significant at $p < .001$. It showed if a member of the informal support network was involved in caring for an elder after (s)he left the hospital, there was a .30 increase in the possibility of an elder using community-based services. This is very interesting because if a person lives with someone, there is a negative relationship (-.41) with using services. However, if there is a family member, friend, or neighbor who cares for the elder after a hospital stay, they are more likely to use formal support services. While the informal support systems are important factors in interactions with the formal support system that is available, it seems as if the interactions are based on subtle distinctions within the informal support system. The incongruence may be explained by the fact that an elder who has been in the hospital may be referred to the community-based resources by hospital staff. On the other hand, an elder who lives with someone and has not been in a hospital has not been in contact with the formal support system, i.e., the hospital, so no referrals are made to other components of the formal support system. In the results seen on table 5.4, having been in the hospital within the last year is highly related to use of services ($p < .0001$).

Another finding that is of interest and that has policy implications is the consistent negative relationship between income and use of services. This means that the elders with higher incomes tend to use fewer services. This phenomenon may be explained by the "positive good" economic theory which explains the use of certain goods only when consumers have no income. As income rises, use of these goods is seen as unnecessary. Another possibility is that use of services is based on income levels and not on need. In some cases people may pay privately and do not consider the help as being in one of the listed categories.

Because the relation between the level of income and use of services is negative, one of the policy implications is that services may be perceived as "welfare," and hence those elders with higher levels of income will not take advantage of these services. Related questions include: What strategies have been successfully employed to attract people who have higher income to use services? Another aspect of the same issue is, do policy makers want to make all services equally available to those that can afford to pay for services and those who cannot? Will developing farther reaching advertising strategies create the "Donald Trump" syndrome, i.e., even he is qualified to receive Social Security, and, if so, is this a desired goal?

VI

Policy Implications

INTRODUCTION

This exploratory study has examined the similarities and differences among Hispanic elders, Mexican Americans, Cuban Americans and Puerto Ricans, in their use of formal support systems. The research indicates that, as a group, Hispanic elders utilize formal support services at a level which is inconsistent with their identified needs. Similarly, Zambrana et al. (1979)[1] found that although Hispanics in East Harlem were twice as impaired as other groups in their study, the otherwise excellent health care organizations had "not seriously addressed themselves to the linguistic and cultural reality of the urban ethnic Puerto Rican," (p 308). Although debatable, as a rule, policies in public institutions are developed to be responsive to perceived need. Yet, according to Lopez (1991),[2] "Despite the need, most older Hispanics do not appear to be participating in social service programs" (p 53).

This research supports and reinforces findings that Hispanic elders remain in the community with high levels of functional and cognitive limitations.[3] This research has focused on three Hispanic groups to determine whether their socio-demographic characteristics play a role in the differences and similarities in use of these community-based services, i.e., the formal system. It is important to begin this discussion since Hispanic poverty and its resultant differences in levels of education, utilization of community-based services and income have not been addressed by other important studies.

This chapter discusses the policy implications of the major research findings and summarizes hypotheses that were supported as well as those that differed from the initial expectations. It concludes with suggestions for future research. It also presents a model for training the "street level bureaucrat."[4]

POLICY ANALYSIS APPROACH

The discussion on policy implications must begin with the question of whether policy makers should develop universal or "exceptionalist" policies (Moroney 1981).[5] Universal policies are designed to apply equitably to all potential recipients across the board. Given Zambrana's (1980), and Lopez', (1991)[6] findings, it is safe to state that universal policies have not met the needs of Hispanic elders and have failed this group of elders. Limited use of community-based services leads one to conclude that they are excluded from the receipt of available community-based aging services. Minority elders are not part of the formal support system circuit and not well integrated into existing society. While there is no stated intent to do so, the end result, use of 1.1 service per Hispanic elder, is one of exclusion, not of inclusion.

In light of these results, a more effective alternative may be to develop exceptionalist policies that target specific populations according to ethnic differences. Moroney, (1981)[7] however, argues that "exceptionalistic services tend to stigmatize, to divide, and to create barriers to community, cooperation, mutual aid, and collective responsibility," (p 94). This, he asserts, runs counter to creating an integrative society. In a similar vein, Dibner, (1981)[8] warns that identifying the elderly as a separate group weakens the family group identity.

This study supports findings that despite being vulnerable to the ravages of age, Hispanic elders are simply not accessing community-based services that are available to them. Therefore, providing services that specifically target minority elders is doing what universal policies have failed to do, i.e., to provide needed services.

KEY FINDINGS AND IMPLICATIONS

This study indicated that of Hispanics 65 years and older, the 26 percent who are frail are particularly vulnerable to what Juarez calls a "cataclysmic" situation in the provision of services unless their needs are considered in the formulation and implementation of policies. Significant differences in socio-demographic characteristics and utilization rates were found among the three groups. However, when policies that address the needs of the aging have been developed, these differences have been glossed over or ignored. As a consequence, existing aging policies fail to address the needs of all their intended targeted population. Herein lies the policy dilemma.

The following differences among the three Hispanic groups are important in the formulation of social policy:

> Mexican American and Cuban American elders have greater incomes than Puerto Ricans. Puerto Ricans have significantly less income than the other two groups. Cuban Americans have higher incomes than either of the other two groups. However, only 13 percent of the Cuban Americans are in the high-income category.

> In the area of ADL limitations, Puerto Ricans are more functionally limited than the two other groups. Cuban Americans have the fewest functional limitations. This pattern holds in the frail category.

> Mexican Americans and Puerto Ricans differed from Cuban Americans on IADL limitations. Cuban Americans have the fewest cognitive limitations.

> Puerto Ricans use more community-based services than either Cuban Americans or Mexican Americans.

> There were no significant differences among the three groups in age or in the utilization of the informal support system that cared for the respondents after hospitalization.

> Income, self-perceived poor health, living with someone, and hospitalization are significant factors in the use of community-based services. The significant

negative interaction between income and use of community-based services suggests that increased income results in a decrease in utilization of community-based services. The presence of someone in the household also has a significant negative interaction with use of community-based services. However, Puerto Ricans differed from the other two groups in that frailty had a strong relation to the use of community-based services. This finding supports the overall research theory that the ethnic groups are different in their use of services.

Increasingly, research on Mexican Americans elders indicates, that they do not get involved with community organizations (Markides et al., 1983).[10] They are also less likely to interact with friends and neighbors; they have fewer confidants and hence tend to be more isolated. The findings reported here also indicate that they are less likely than the other two groups of elders to interact with formal service providers. These findings are consistent with Markides'[11] findings. Research on Mexican American elders and frequency of contact with their children is mixed. Markides et al. (1983) found no difference in frequency of contact with children between Mexican American and their White counterparts. However, Weeks and Cuellar (1981), and Lubben and Becerra (1987)[12] found that Mexican American elders had more frequent contacts with their children than other elders. (Lubben and Becerra[13] actually found that both Mexican American and Chinese American elders had high rates of interaction with their children.)

The findings describe a situation where, of the three major Hispanic elderly groups, only Puerto Ricans use services when they are frail. In light of these results, it is particularly important to target programs to equitably address the needs of all frail elders.

ISSUES IN SERVICE DELIVERY

In addition to differences among the three groups, other factors distinguish Hispanic elders from the majority group elders. These differences also need be considered when developing aging program policies. Hispanics, as a group, do have certain dissimilar characteristics from elders of the majority culture. These factors are influenced by an individual's degree of assimilation (Schur, Albers and Berk, 1995). Two major characteristics are relevant.

Cultural Differences

Mexican and other Hispanic elders' lifetime cultural experiences are important to those who depend on social and public institutions (Maldonado, 1979).[14] These cultural experiences are different from elders of the majority culture. One important aspect of the Hispanic experience that Maldonado identifies is "cultural incongruence" (p 182), found in social and public institutions. He claims that because institutions reflect the values of the dominant power, they by definition are not responsive to the needs of minority cultures: "This cultural incongruence has resulted in large-scale misunderstandings, ineffectiveness, underutilization, and human suffering" (p 182). This is so due to the inability or reluctance of minority elders to use services that do not respond to them in a culturally sensitive manner.

Language Differences

Although the inability to speak English is not significant in the use of services, the fact that 87 percent of this sample completed the survey in Spanish is a significant indicator of language preference. In one study regarding the role that speaking Spanish plays in use of services, Higginbotham et al. (1991)[15] found that being interviewed in Spanish was highly predictive of the utilization of a *curandero* (See Appendix B), indicating that individuals may experience difficulty communicating in English with health professionals. Therefore, they may use a community medical system in which they can communicate in their preferred language. According to Solis et al. (1991),[16] language preference can be seen as both an indicator of cultural and functional integration. These results support the need to provide culturally sensitive services to Hispanic elders because they are not part of the larger dominant and integrated society.

These results reported in this study do not indicate that the inability to speak English is a factor in the use of community-based services. Nevertheless, failure to speak in the dominant language leads to non-participation by elderly Hispanics in the larger society and to cultural incongruence on the part of institutions meant to assist these populations. Lacayo (1980)[17] referred to this as the "salience of culture" concluding that older Hispanics prefer to be served by institutional representatives who both speak their language and are familiar with their culture.

This research raises questions regarding the dynamics of the Hispanic elders and their majority-culture environment. By default, and perhaps to some degree by design, many services are simply not available to elderly Hispanics. To continue in the current mode means to perpetuate existing exclusionary policies.

Another issue that plays a significant role in the use of health care services by Mexican American elders is the restrictive Medicaid policies in some states. For example, 30 percent of the Mexican American population reside in Texas, and Texas ranks thirty-third out of 35 states with programs for the medically needy (GAO, 1992),[18] meaning that its eligibility criteria for access to health services by poor people are among the most stringent. This seriously impacts use of services by Mexican Americans and may be a factor in their overall low use of services.

The main thrust of the research was to find similarities and differences among the three ethnic groups of Hispanic elders so that policies that address these populations would be more culturally responsive. Therefore, the policy analysis approach is to elaborate on the policy recommendations stemming from the findings of this research.

It is possible that the different definitions for frail that the formal system applies to all populations may be inappropriate as the definitions apply to elderly Hispanics. If this is so, could the disparity in applying this definition to the Hispanic elder contribute to the observed low utilization of health services and nursing homes? Perhaps this as well as other definitions may be inappropriate for some cultural groups or for groups where extended family is available. This finding is even more interesting given that previous studies have found that Hispanic elders say they are frail or ill at an earlier age than other groups (Chase 1990).[19]

In essence, the Hispanic elders meet the definition of frailty based on activities of daily living and instrumental activities of daily living limitations at twice the rate as they see themselves in the "poor" self-reported health category. Culturally, it is possible that the elders are not under-utilizing services but that the level of frailty and utilization rates are being measured by a culturally inappropriate measuring stick. It could also mean that their self-perception differs from the objective criteria that are used by the formal system to evaluate all elders. Differences in how words are used change when those words are translated. Also, the context of the words may change when cultures are different from one another. Therefore, language differences need to be given close attention in future research.

IMPLICATIONS FOR POLICY

It is important to note that 46 percent of the 2,019 participants in this study did not use any services. Previous studies indicate that Mexican Americans use less health care services than all other Hispanic groups.[20] However, when asked to identify the type of services needed, 33 percent of the respondents needed food stamps and 15 percent needed home visiting nurses. Food stamps are already the most widely used service so perhaps the use should even be higher. However, visiting nurse services are the least used service and perhaps their availability is not known. According to Carp.[21] "One problem with services to older people is the discrepancy between provision and utilization. The gap between provision and use may be even greater when an additional factor–membership in a minority group–is operative," (p 1). This research supports her conclusions for community-based services.

Elderly Hispanics have received little attention over the last 30 years. The formal support systems, whether at the policy or programmatic level, have made little effort to integrate them. The assumptions that Hispanics "take care of their own" and "refuse to speak English" have led to the development of color-blind policies. The society, however, is neither color-blind nor equitable.

A consideration that complicates the development of exceptionalistic policies is the anticipated results from effective targeting strategies. The expected positive result of targeting is that elders receive much-needed services. This would possibly free limited family resources to meet other pressing family needs. Additionally, as the number of ethnic consumers increases, the system might become more culturally responsive, conceivably leading to even more increased utilization of community-based services.

On the other hand, a move to bring services to Hispanics, and particularly to Mexican American elders, could impact *la familia*. Ascribed roles that elders have occupied in the family system would conceivably change. For example, the re-telling of cultural stories and the teaching of values to grand- and great-grandchildren (such as to care for frail individuals) could be eliminated from the culture should elders be encouraged to use the formal support system. The formal social support system would perform services that were previously performed by family members. Changes could also occur by elders leaving the home to attend functions instead of remaining in the home with the family.

The push and pull, or yin and yang, of the development of exceptionalist policies brings to focus the trade-offs that many minority people undertake in order to be part of the integrative society mentioned by Moroney (1981).[22] In other words, Hispanic minority elders and their families experience both positive and negative results as they become integrated into the larger society.

RECOMMENDATIONS

These recommendations are based on findings reflecting similarities and differences among the three groups. First, the similarities among the three groups. Perhaps the one most important similarity among the Hispanic cultures is their difference from the majority culture. The behaviors of Hispanic elders are dictated by the manner in which they view themselves in relation to family and the outside world that is different. By birth and subsequent life course experiences, they find themselves in a family system where members are interdependent. The social exchanges that take place permit the micro-system, i.e., *la familia*, to continue.

As if to further reinforce the inter-generational interdependence and non-participation in external services, the majority of these elders speak Spanish. Unless Spanish is spoken by community service providers, there is little opportunity to increase the numbers of consumers. This study has shown that Hispanic elders on the average, use only one community-based service. Yet, as previously mentioned, up to 33 percent of the sample identified needs for some of these services. Therefore, if Lacayo (1980), Chase (1990), and Higginbotham (1991)[23] are correct, the needs of these elders would be better served by facilitating access to services in Spanish. Also, services could be located within the *barrios* so that transportation issues become less problematic to both services delivery and service access.

Given the interesting finding from these data that speaking English was not an important factor in the use of community-based services, language becomes a variable that needs to be further explored. Would speaking English facilitate the use of services by the 33 percent who identified the need for some of the services? Or is the reverse more true? That is, if services are provided by Spanish-speaking personnel, the cultural incongruence factor is overcome to some degree, thus facilitating higher use of services? In general, bilingual capability needs to be researched regarding its role in the use of services.

The majority of all Hispanics continue to experience low income and low levels of education. Future generations must be better prepared to be labor force participants in other than blue collar or low paying jobs. More effective educational strategies are extremely important in improving these socio-economic areas. Ironically, it is predicted that as more Hispanic elders have higher incomes, their demand for community-based or publicly assisted services will decrease. A positive change in economic status will ensure that Hispanic elders who elect not to be integrated into the larger society will have real economic choices regarding service consumption. However, a concerted effort to educate the younger generation is a prerequisite to having real economic choices.

Stigma is another factor which may lead to underutilization of services among the three Hispanic groups. One way of attracting underserved consumers is to use Spanish media to change the idea that these services are welfare-type services. Stigma is an important point to clarify because Hispanics have a great deal of pride and want to be self-sufficient (Marin and Marin 1992; Weeks and Cuellar 1981).[24] There are at least two levels on which to address the stigma issue. First, the results indicate that as income increases, use of community-based services declines. A quick inference may be made that similar services are being purchased. However, this inference is quickly dismissed when one looks at the private-for-profit organizations that deliver aging services. Except for nursing services, none of the other nine services described in this study has been provided by entrepreneurial enterprises. Therefore, it is likely that some Hispanic elders do not utilize services because of the stigma attached to the use of services.

The second level of stigma may be explained from Moroney's[25] scenario which identifies exceptionalistic policies as stigmatizing. I argue that because these elders are not receiving needed services, what started out as purported universal policies became exceptionalistic policies once implemented. Therefore, failure to adequately deliver services to these populations, creates it's own stigma–that of exclusion. Accordingly, outreach to these communities must incorporate communication with existing ethnic groups and ethnic leaders. It is important to use existing networks.

This section offers recommendations on similar factors in the use of community-based services. Because living with someone is a significant inverse predictor of service use, those elders with limited informal support systems may need assistance in their care-receiving activities. This can be done with minimum damage to the natural support system by hiring minority or bilingual/bicultural staff and training non-minority staff (Chase 1990).[26] Sensitivity and respect for these elders can be encouraged by the provision of training opportunities.

Age and being in poor health are two other factors that have a positive relation to use of services. In order to strategically address these areas, knowledge of constituents is important. Services can best be planned and delivered to maximize utilization if agencies know who the recipients are. It is likely that people in either or both of these categories will not be very visible in the community. Therefore, it is important that local ethnic leaders, ethnic groups, or church officials be asked to help identify these individuals. The "snowball method" can be applied to this process of identifying the elders. (The snowball method asks a community informant to identify one or more respondents who in turn are asked to identify more respondents. This process is continued until the desired numbers of respondents are identified.) Using this and other possible approaches may help bring services to frail elders who would otherwise be very isolated.

The recommendations that come from these analyses involve the formal support system at the level that is closest to the respondents, i.e., the direct service level. A tool was designed to train street level bureaucrats, front line staff, and intake workers on selected characteristics of Mexican American elders. Such a tool is important because this type of client comprehensive assessment is not ordinarily available in the training of front line staff.

The Assimilation Assessment Model (see table 6.0) has six cultural characteristics on the left hand column that can be assessed on a continuum from traditional to non-traditional behaviors. The model can be used with Mexican Americans clients to assess whether the individual could best be assisted by a bilingual/bicultural staff person. The table can be used as a training tool to sensitize staff to differences that are found within one of the groups (Mexican Americans) that is the focus of this research. Knowing that people are indeed different may assist agencies in diminishing their cultural incongruence.

In table 6.0, it is important to note that most people of minority cultures usually exhibit behaviors and characteristics that float in multiple directions within the table. It would be unusual to find a person who would describe him/herself as fitting completely under one column. As a matter of fact, every user of the tool should be cautioned to avoid putting people into any one category.

The table is intended to be completed by the consumer. The Mexican American client should be given time to assess where (s)he is on the continuum prior to the institutional representative making generalizations about the consumer from the way a person talks, dresses, or from socio-demographic information. This approach should produce several benefits:

1. It empowers the client by giving him/her the right to define him/herself to the agency;

2. It reflects respect and acceptance of the client's ability to provide self-identification other than by institutionally required data;

3. This self-identification provides the public institution a more honest assessment of its clientele. This data could lead to more appropriate staff training, resource allocation, appropriate program development, and staff recruitment and training.

Table 6.0
Assimilation Assessment Model

	Traditional	Somewhat Traditional	Somewhat Non-Traditional	Non-Traditional
Spiritual or Religious	Usually Catholic adhere to teachings.	Attend church with regularity.	Church attendance is more sporadic.	Possibly not involved.
Family	Close-knit immediate and extended family. Strong patriarchal family.	Very connected with immediate family. Father and mother share decision-making role.	Immediate family may live in another geographic area. Adult children may be consulted in making decisions.	See family infrequently. Adult children are expected to make independent decisions.
Social	Social Activities revolve around family and church.	Less involved with church and extended family.	No church activity and little with extended family.	Infrequently attend family gatherings.

Table 6.0 Continued
Assimilation Assessment Model

Eating	Prefer to eat with tortillas and eat traditional foods.	More variety in diet and frequent use of eating utensils.	Less traditional foods.	Little to no traditional foods or traditional foods are store bought.
Language	Speak in Spanish	Prefer to speak Spanish, particularly at home but speak some English. Count in Spanish	Is bilingual and may mix Spanish and English within sentences.	May be bilingual but prefer to speak English, think and count in English
Health	Use herbs teas and curandero (natural healer) as initial resource.	Use herbs and teas; if not better in one or two days call doctor.	Self-administer across-the-counter medicines and will call doctor.	Call doctor if self-administered medicine is not effective. Accept physical explanations for illness.

Sara Aleman, 1996

CONCLUSIONS

The heterogeneity of the Hispanic elders is a challenge to policy makers. The differences, however, are not so great that creative policy makers cannot develop culturally appropriate policies that provide immediate benefits to constituents. There are already some approaches used by private consultants to train management teams on dealing with a multi-cultural labor force. Learning from what has already been developed is important during this time of fiscal restraint. It is important for each agency to develop strategies for working with multi-cultural consumers. Developing policies that effectively provide multi-cultural groups with needed services is long overdue.

Another strategy that can be employed is to target Mexican American communities to receive information on services that are available. In particular, this group is singled out because of its low level of utilization of community-based services and because the predictive models tested in this research seem to less strongly identify what factors contribute to use of services by Mexican Americans.

FUTURE RESEARCH

The questions that face policy makers and service providers are numerous and need to be addressed. Answering them may change the reality of those communities that have been denied the benefits of the society. Research that examines how these poor, under-educated elders manage to remain in the community with such little use of formal support services needs to be further developed. The strengths that enable these elders to survive can be used by policy makers to assist them, their families, and all elders. Qualitative studies that examine the family systems and the evolution of *la familia* can best get at these strengths. Additionally, it is important to realize that the proximity of the Mexican border means that immigrants will continue to come to the United States. The continuous flow of new immigrants will require the use of bilingual/bicultural staff to assist with services. Qualitative research can uncover information that can reveal values that may be constant and those that may be changing as minority families become assimilated. This is particularly important for planning purposes. As the total aged population increases, Hispanic elders may have to compete even more with other aged populations for limited resources. To assist Hispanic family systems and to continue to keep the elders in the community, formal and family resources must complement each other. The Hispanic cultures may be helpful as models for developing policies that keep families intact. Another important area that qualitative research may target is the relationship that may exist between service utilization and English language skills. If not speaking English is not a barrier to service utilization, what is?

Additionally, quantitative research needs to be carried out with data sets that study elderly Hispanics as different groups, with different strengths and different needs. Questions about the definitive role that speaking Spanish plays in the use of services need to be further examined. This research showed that there is no relation between the use of community-based services and the ability to speak English. However, what would happen if these seniors knew about services and experienced linguistic and cultural identification with the service providers? Pilot programs could be developed to explore attitudes, behaviors, and family dynamics that such endeavors would produce.

Clearly, the low adjusted R square for the Mexican American population model indicates the need for further research that examines family, health, and community-systems as predictors of use of services. This population could also benefit from more research on its psychological view of the non-Hispanic world. Further, given its current isolation from the general population, will the family system change with the incessant onslaught from the non-Hispanic larger society?

Research also needs to address changes in family composition and its impact on care of elders. There is some evidence that Hispanic families are becoming smaller. It also makes sense to say that larger families have larger informal support systems. What is in store for Hispanic elders who have fewer children and become dependent on a smaller informal support system? Some of these questions can best be answered by analyzing representative samples of the different populations. It is especially important to examine if Mexican Americans and Cuban Americans are different from Puerto Ricans as they become more dependent on others due to functional and cognitive limitations. There is evidence that some Puerto Ricans return to their birthplace once they are elderly. While some Cuban Americans think that one day they may return to Cuba from their exile, the possibility seems less likely as the years go by. Some Mexican immigrants do not learn English nor do they make efforts to become naturalized citizens because they hope to be able to return "home." However, as their children grow up in the United States, with different values the pull is to remain where the children are. All of this describes elders that are different in their choices, their dreams, and very possibly in the way that they define themselves in the environment. These populations will increase and public agencies must learn to respond to these groups with culturally appropriate policies.

Notes

[1] Ruth E., Zambrana Rolando Merino and Sarah Santana, *Health Services and the Puerto Rican Elderly* (1979; New York: Springer Publishing Company) 308-319.

[2] Christina Lopez, 53.

[3] The researchers Louise Woerner, 1979, and John R. Weeksand Jose B. Cuellar, 1979, look at the high levels of limitations that Hispanic elders have.

[4] Michael Lipsky, 1980.

[5] This author, Robert M. Moroney, 1981, discusses the potential negative impact of exceptionalist policies.

[6] See notes 1 and 2 above.

[7] See note 5 above.

[8] Andrew Dibner, 193-195.

[9] Rumaldo Juarez, 69-93.

[10] Kyriakos S. Markides, Harry W. Martin with Ernesto Gomez, 1983.

[11] Ibid.

[12] James E. Lubben and Rosina M. Becerra, 130-144; John R. Weeks and Jose B. Cuellar, 388-394.

[13] Ibid.

[14] David Maldonado, 135-141.

[15] Higginbotham et al., 1991, found that speaking Spanish may be highly predictive of using a *curandero.*

[16] Julia Solis, Gary Marks, Melinda Garcia and David Shelton, 1991, found language preference to be an indicator of integration.

[17] Lacayo, 1980, presents an interesting discussion on "salience of culture."

[18] GAO, 1-26.

[19] Richard A. Chase, *Minority Elders in Minnesota* (1990 Minneapolis: Wilder Research Center).

[20] Antonia Estrada, 27-31; John C. Higginbotham, 32-35.

[21] See note 1 above.

[22] Moroney, 1981.

[23] Chase, (1990), Lacayo (1980) and Higginbotham, (1991) all propose that services be available in Spanish.

[24] Marin and Marin, 1992, and Weeks and Cuellar, 1981, researched the importance of stigma to Hispanic elders.

[25] Robert A. Moroney made the relationship between exceptionalist policies and stigma.

[26] Chase, 18.

Appendix A

FRAILTY DEFINITION BY SELECTED STATES

Oregon

Requires complex medication or treatment procedures 3 or more times a week

       or

Requires rehabilitation therapies 5 or more times per week (physical, occupational, speech)

       or

Need for assistance or dependence in one of five clusters:
>*Mobility cluster*: Mobility, transfer
>*Continence cluster*: Toileting, bladder continence, bowel continence
>*Bathing cluster*: Bathing, personal hygiene
>*Grooming cluster*: Grooming, dressing
>*Behavior cluster*: Orientation, adaptation to change, judgment, memory, awareness of needs, wandering, danger to self/others, behavioral demands on others

       The Oregon rules list these minimum criteria for being deemed dependent or needing assistance in each cluster: Mobility - needs assistance (not totally dependent) in mobility or transfer (may be

117

independent in the other); Continence - needs assistance in toileting, bladder continence, or bowel continence (may be independent in two of the three); Bathing - needs assistance or has total dependence in bathing, *or* total dependence in personal hygiene; Grooming - needs assistance in dressing or has total dependence in dressing, *or* has total dependence in grooming; Behavior - a series of complex formulas determines dependence or need for assistance in this cluster. Essentially, a person is considered dependent or needing assistance if he/she scores dependent in at least two of the eight items (may be independent in the other six) or dependent in one and needing assistance in another (may be independent in the remaining six).

Connecticut

5-6 ADL dependencies (total or partial)

> or

Available, willing, and able caregiver but caregiver's age is age 75 or older, or no caregiver present, or caregiver is not available, willing, or able for *all* of the applicant's needs
> and
One of the following:
> 2-4 (out of 6) ADL dependencies (total or partial)
> 4-8 (out of 8) IADL dependencies (total or partial)
> 4-10 errors on the mental status questionnaire
> Wandering

> or

> Abusive/assaultive behavior
> and
One of the following:
> 2-4 (out of six) ADL dependencies (total or partial)
> 4-8 (out of 8) IADL dependencies (total or partial)
> 4-10 errors on the mental status questionnaire

The Connecticut rules utilize the six ADLs of bathing, dressing, toileting, transfer, continence (bowel and bladder), and feeding. They specify the eight IADLs of shopping, using transportation, medication management, laundry, meal preparation, light housework, using the telephone, and managing finances.

Virginia

Totally dependent in 2-4 (out of 7) ADLS
    and
Problems in behavioral/orientation
    and
Difficulties in medication administration
    or
Totally dependent in 2-4 (out of 7) ADLs
    and
Problems in behavior orientation
    and
Uncorrected instability or immobility (joint motion problems)
    or
Totally dependent on 5-7 (out of 7) ADLs
    and
Partially dependent in 2-7 ADLs
    and
Dependent in outdoor mobility
    and
Problems in behavior/orientation
    and
Medical condition requiring nursing care
    or
Skilled care general medical management on a continuing basis (as an alternative to hospital care)

The Virginia rules list seven ADLs: bathing, dressing, toileting, transfer, bladder continence, bowel continence, and eating/feeding. Specified problems in behavior/orientation are wandering passive behavior, abusive/aggressive/disruptive behavior, and disorientation.

Persons who require medication administration by a licensed/professional nurse and/or require medication monitoring at least weekly are deemed to have difficulties in medication administration.

New York

Requires more than occasional supervision in any ADL
　　　and
No appropriate housing available

　　　　or

Inadequate informal supports
　　　and
One of the following:
　　　Totally dependent in 4 (out of 4) ADLs or comatose
　　　Partially dependent in 1 (out of 4) ADLs and one of the following:
　　　History of unpredictable behaviors
　　　Restorative services needed and not available/accessible on an outpatient basis
　　　Skilled services or constant monitoring of a medical condition

In the New York rules, four ADLs are identified: mobility, transfer, continence, and eating.

Appendix B

GLOSSARY

Chicano: a term that emerged in the middle to late 1960s to denote a politically aware and potentially active individual of Mexican American descent. There are numerous explanations of the origin of the term, but there does not seem to be one explanation that is embraced by all. It still continues to represent the same meaning, but it is primarily a self-identifier used by younger rather than older cohorts of Mexican Americans (Becerra 1988, 145).

Curandero: a folk medicine healer.

Cuban: this is a person who was born in Cuba and who now resides in the United States. In this study a person who makes the distinction that he/she is Cuban and not Cuban American is a person who is foreign born.

Cuban American: a person who was born in the United States and whose ancestors came from Cuba.

Formal Support Network or Formal System: the social services or other community-based support that is paid for by the recipient. It is oftentimes a system that is set in place by governmental entities to assist certain targeted groups, i.e., elderly, mentally retarded, abused children, etc. The services included in a formal system will usually vary from state to state, region to region, and rural to urban areas. This variation is partly due to the different available services which can be found in different geographic areas, and partly due to criteria employed by funding sources for eligibility. Population base, the local economy, and political power may all influence the money which comes into the locale to develop the formal support network that is then available to residents.

Informal Support Network or Informal System: This includes the assistance that elders receive from family, friends, and neighbors. This is usually unpaid assistance. Many studies have found that the support which is provided by the informal support system/network is at least 80 percent of the total assistance that elders receive.

La Familia "family": an extended multigenerational group of persons, among whom specific social roles were ascribed. Mutual support, sustenance, and interaction among family members during both work and leisure hours dominated the lives of persons in these traditional Mexican families (Becerra 1988, 147).

Mexican: for the purpose of this research, this is a person who was born in Mexico and who now resides in the United States. In this study a person who makes the distinction that he/she is Mexican and not Mexican American is a person who is foreign born.

Mexican American: a person who was born in the United States and whose ancestors came from Mexico.

Puerto Rican: a person who was born in Puerto Rico. They are United States citizens regardless of whether they were born in the island or on the mainland.

Social Support: giving and receiving of any of the possible range of human contacts, interactions or services, whether instrumental, expressive, or multidimensional in nature. This process enables older individuals to maintain themselves, despite change, so that needs of various kinds are met and, further, so that their sense of self and meaning in the world can endure (Rubenstein 1985, 166).

Social Support System: a pattern of continuous or intermittent ties and interchanges of mutual assistance that plays significant role in maintaining the psychological, social, and physical integrity of the individual over time, (Rubenstein 1985, 167).

References

Bassford, Tamsen L. 1995. "Health Status of Hispanic Elders." In David V. Espino (Guest Ed.), *Clinics in Geriatric Medicine.* Philadelphia: W.B. Saunders Company.

Bastida, Elena. 1979. "Family Integration in Later Life Among Hispanic Americans." *Journal of Minority Aging* 4: 42-49.

Becerra Rosina M. 1983. "The Mexican-American: Aging in a Changing Culture." In R.L. McNeely and John L. Cohen (Eds), *Aging in Minority Groups.* Beverly Hills: Sage Publications: 108-118.

— . 1988. "The Mexican American Family." In Charles H. Mindel, Robert W. Habenstein and Roosevelt Wright, Jr. (Eds), *Ethnic Families in America: Patterns and Variations*, 3d ed. New York: Elsevier Science Publishing Co., Inc.: 1-15.

Bengston, Vern L. 1979. "Ethnicity and Perceptions of Aging." Presented at the Conference on Aging: A Challenge to Science and Social Policy. Vichy, France.

Butler, Robert N., Myrna Lewis, and Trey Sunderland 1991. *Aging and Mental Health: Positive Psychosocial and Biomedical Approaches.* New York: MacMillan Publishing Company.

Cantor, Marjorie. 1979. "The Informal Support System of New York's Inner City Elderly: Is Ethnicity a Factor?" In Donald E. Gelfand and Alfred J. Kutzikn (Eds.), *Ethnicity and Aging: Theory, Research and Policy.* New York: Springer Publishing Company: 153-174.

— . 1980. "The Informal Support System: Its Relevance in the Lives of the Elderly." In Edgar F. Birgatta and Neil G. McCluskey (Eds), *Aging and Society: Current Research and Policy Perspectives.* Beverly Hills: Sage Publications: 131-143.

Carp, Frances M. 1968. *Factors in Utilization of Services by the Mexican-American Elderly*. Palo Alto, CA: American Institutes for Research.

— . 1983. "Social Care for the Aged in the United States: Issues and Challenges." In Shura Saul (Ed.), *Groupwork With the Frail Elderly*. New York: The Haworth Press: 13-20.

Chase, Richard A. 1990. *Minority Elders in Minnesota*. (Minneapolis: Wilder Research Center, Amherst H. Wilder Foundation) (March).

Children's Defense Fund. 1991. *The State of America's Children 1991*. Washington, D.C.: Children's Defense Fund.

Commonwealth Fund Commission Report. 1989. *Poverty and Poor Health Among Elderly Hispanic Americans*. Baltimore: The Commonwealth Fund Commission.

Congressional Budget Office. 1989. *Staff Working Papers: The Economic Status of the Elderly*. Washington, D.C. (May). Cuellar, Israel, Lorwen C. Harris, and Ricardo Jasso. 1980. "An Acculturation Scale for Mexican American Normal and Clinical Populations." *Hispanic Journal of Behavioral Sciences* 2(3): 199-217.

Cuellar, Jose. 1981. "Introduction." In E. Percil Stanford and Shirley A. Lockery (Eds.), *Trends and Status of Minority Aging*. San Diego State University: University Center on Aging, College of Human Services: 1-3.

— . 1988. "The Ethnography of Hispanic Aging." In Steven R. Applewhite (Ed.), *The Hispanic Elderly in Transition*. Westport, CT: Greenwood Press: 171-187.

— . 1990. *Aging and Health: Hispanic American Elders*. Stanford, CA: Stanford Geriatric Education Center, SGEC Working Paper Series, Number 5.

Daley, John Michael, Steven R. Applewhite, and James Jorquez. 1989. "Community Participation of the Chicano Elderly: A Model." *International Journal Aging and Human Development* 29:2:135-150.

Dibner, Andrew S. 1981. "Ethnic and Cultural Variations in the Care of the Aged: Introduction." *Hispanic Elderly* 193-195.

Dowd, James J. and Vern L. Bengston. 1978. "Aging in Minority Populations: An Examination of the Double Jeopardy Hypothesis." *Journal of Gerontology* 33 (3): 427-436.

Enchautegui, María E. 1995.*Policy Implications of Latino Poverty.* Washington, D.C.: The Urban Institute.

Estrada, Antonio L., Fernando M. Trevino, and Laura A. Ray. 1990. "Health Care Utilization Barriers Among Mexican Americans: Evidence from HHANES 1982-84." *American Journal of Public Health* (December) Vol. 80, Supplement: 27-31.

Gelfand, Donald E. 1982. *Aging, the Ethnic Factor.* Boston: Little, Brown and Company.

Ginzberg, Eli. 1991. "Access to Health Care for Hispanics." *JAMA* (January) 265:2:238-241.

Gratton, Brian. 1987. "Familism Among the Black and Mexican-American Elderly: Myth or Reality?" *Journal of Aging Studies* 1 (1) 19-32.

Greenstein, Robert. 1988. *Shortchanged: Recent Developments in Hispanic Poverty, Income and Employment.* (Washington, D. C.: Center on Budget and Policy Priorities, November 1).

Greene, Vernon L. and Deborah J. Monahan. 1984. "Comparative Utilization of Community Based Long-Term Care Services by Hispanic and Anglo Elderly in a Case Management System. *Jounal of Gerontology* 39 (6): 730-735.

Harel, Zev. 1987. "Older Americans Act Related Homebound Aged: What Difference Does Racial Background Make?" *Ethnicity and Gerontological Social Work.* New York: Haworth Press, Inc.: 133-143.

Harel, Zev, Ed McKinney, and Michael Williams. 1987. "Aging, Ethnicity, and Services: Empirical and Theoretical Perspectives." In Donald E. Gelfand and Charles M. Barresi (Eds.), *Ethnic Dimensions in Aging.* New York: Springer Publishing Company: 196-210.

Henderson, J. Neil. 1992. "The Need for Cultural Sensitivity in Working with Ethnic Minority Elderly." In Marcela Gutierrez-Mayka, J. Neil Henderson and Eileen F. Poiley (Eds.) Ethnic Minority Elderly: Better Understanding for Better Care. Tampa, FL: Univerisity of South Florida Geriatric Education Center.

— . 1993. *Ethnic and Cultural Issues in Long Term Care of Minority Elderly.* Tampa, FL: National Eldercare Institute on Long Term Care and Alzheimer's Disease at the Suncoast Gerontology Center.

Higginbotham, John C., Fernando M. Trevino, and Laura A. Ray. 1990. "Utilization of Curanderos by Mexican Americans: Prevalence and Predictors Findings from HHANES 1982-84." *American Journal of Public Health* (December) Vol. 80, Supplement: 32-35.

Hopper, Susan V. 1993. "The Influence of Ethnicity on the Health of Older Women." In Fran E. Kaiser (Guest Ed.), *Clinics in Geriatric Medicine*, (February) Philadelphia, PA.: W.B. Saunders Company.

Jackson, James. 1970. "Aged Negros: Their Cultural Departures from Statistical Stereotypes and Rural-Urban Differences." *Gerontologist* 10: 140-145.

Juarez, Rumaldo Z. 1986-1987. "Current and Future Long-Term Care Needs of Mexican American Elderly in Arizona." In *Renato Rosaldo Lecture Series* 4:69-93.

Kantrowitz, Barbara and Lourdes Rosado. 1991. "Falling Further Behind." *Newsweek* (19 August):80.

Lacayo, Carmela G., Jean K. Crawford, Henry Rodriguez, and Ramona Soto. 1980. *A National Study to Assess the Service Needs of the Hispanic Elderly: Final Report.* Los Angeles: Association Nacional Pro Personas Mayores.

Lipsky, Michael. 1980. *Street Level Bureaucracy.* New York: Russel Sage.

Liu, Korbin, Kenneth G. Manton, and Barbara Marzetta Liu. 1985. "Home Care Expenses for the Disabled Elderly." *Health Care Financing Review* (winter)7:2:51-58.

Lopez, Christina. 1991. *On the Sidelines: Hispanic Elderly and the Continuum of Care.* National Council of La Raza, Policy Analysis Center and Office of Institutional Development, Washington, D.C.

Lubben, James E. 1988. "Assessing Social Networks Among Elderly Populations." *Family Community Health* 11 (3) 42-52.

Lubben, James E. and Rosina M. Becerra. 1987. "Social Support Among Black, Mexican, and Chinese Elderly." In Donald E. Gelfand and Charles M. Barresi (Eds.), *Ethnic Dimensions of Aging.* New York: Springer Publishing Company: 130-144.

Maldonado, David. 1988. "El Barrio: Perceptions and Utilization of the Hispanic Neighborhood." In Steven R. Applewhite (Ed.), *The Hispanic Elderly in Transition.* Westport, CT: Greenwood Press: 135-141.

Marin, Geraldo and Barbara VanOss Marin. 1991. *Research with Hispanic Populations*. Newbury Park, CA: Sage Publications.

Markides, Kyriakos S. 1983. "Minority Aging." In M. W. Riley, B. B. Hess, and K. Bond (Eds.), *Aging in Society: Selected Reviews of Recent Research*. Hillsdale, NJ: Lawrence Erlbaum Associates, Inc.: 115-138.

— . 1986. "Minority Status, Aging, and Mental Health." *International Journal of Aging and Human Development* 285-300.

— . 1990. "Predictors of Well-Being and Functioning in Older Mexican Americans and Anglos: An Eight Year Follow-Up." *Journal of Gerontology: Social Sciences* 45:1:S69-S73.

Markides, Kyriakos S., Joanne S. Boldt, Joanne S. and Laura A. Ray. 1986. "Sources of Helping and Intergenerational Solidarity: A Three-Generations Study of Mexican Americans." *Journal of Gerontology* 41:4:506-511.

Markides, Kyriakos S., Jeannine Coreil, and Linda Perkowski Rogers. 1989. "Aging and Health Among Southwestern Hispanics." In Kyriakos S. Markides (Ed.), *Aging and Health*. Sage Publications: Newbury Park, CA.

Markides, Kyriakos S., Jersey Liang, and James S. Jackson. 1990. "Race, Ethnicity, and Aging: Conceptual and Methodological Issues." In Robert H. Binstock and Linda K. George (Eds.), *Handbook of Aging in the Social Sciences*, 3d ed. New York: Academic Press, Inc.: 112-129.

Markides, Kyriakos S., and Harry W. Martin with Ernesto Gomez. 1983. *Older Mexican Americans: A Study In An Urban Barrio*. Austin, Texas: The Center for Mexican American Studies of the University of Texas at Austin.

Mindel, Charles H. 1980. "Extended Familism among Urban Mexican American, Anglos and Blacks." *Hispanic Journal of Behavioral Sciences* 2 (1): 21-34.

Moore, Patricia and Joseph T. Hepworth. 1994. "Use of Perinatal and Infant Health Services by Mexican-American Medicaid Enrollees." *The Journal of the American Medical Association* 272 (4): 297-304.

Moroney, Robert M. 1981. "Policy Analysis Within a Value Theoretical Framework." In Ron Haskins and James J. Gallagher (Eds.), *Models for Analysis of Social Policy*. Norwood, NJ: ABLEX Publishing Corporation: 78-99.

Moore, Patricia and Joseph T. Hepworth. 1994. "Use of Perinatal and Infant Health Services by Mexican-American Medicaid Enrollees." *JAMA* 272 (4): 297-304

Morris, John N. and Sylvia Sherwood. 1984. "Informal Support for Vulnerable Elderly Persons: Can they Be Counted On, Why Do They Work?" *International Journal of Aging and Human Development* 18 (2): 81-98.

O'Sullivan, Michael J. and Bethsabe Lasso. 1992. "Community Mental Health Services for Hispanics: A Test of the Culture Compatibility Hypothesis." *Hispanic Journal of Behavioral Sciences* 14 (4): 455-468.

Penalosa, F. 1968. "Mexican Family Roles." *Journal of Marriage and Family* November: 680-689.

Pousada, Lidia. 1995. "Hispanic-American Elders." In David V. Espino (Guest Ed*)*, *Clinics in Geriatric Medicine*. Philadelphia, PA.: W.B. Saunders Company (February).

Rizzuto, Ana-Marie. 1981. "Ethnic and Cultural Variations in the Care of the Aged Discussion: Hispanic Elderly and Natural Support Systems: A Special Focus on Puerto Ricans." *Hispanic Elderly* 253-255.

Rubinstein, Robert L. 1985. "The Elderly Who Live Alone and Their Social Supports." *Annual Review of Gerontology and Geriatrics* 5: 165-193.

Schur, Claudia L., Leigh Ann Albers and Marc L. Berk. 1995. "Health Care Use by Hispanic Adults: Financial vs. Non-Financial Determinants." *Health Care Financing Review* 17 (2): 71-88.

Sena-Rivera, Jaime. 1979. "Extended Kinship in the United States: Competing Models and the Case of La Familia Chicana." Journal of Marriage and the Family (February): 121-129.

Shanas, Ethel and George L. Maddox. 1985. "Health, Health Resources, and the Utilization of Care." In Robert H. Binstock and Ethel Shanas (Eds.), *Handbook of Aging and the Social Sciences*. New York: Van Nostrand Reinhold Company: 696-726.

Solis, Julia M., Gary Marks, Melinda Garcia, and David Shelton. 1990. "Acculturation, Access to Care, and Use of Preventive Services by Hispanics: Findings from HHANES 1982-84." *American Journal of Public Health* (December) Vol. 80, Supplement: 11-19.

Sotomayor, Marta and Steven R. Applewhite. 1988. "The Hispanic Elderly and the Extended Multigenerational Family." In Steven R.

Applewhite (Ed.), *Hispanic Elderly in Transition: Theory, Research, and Policy and Practice*. Westport, CT: Greenwood Press: 121-133.

Stoller, Eleanor Palo and Rose Campbell Gibson. 1994. *Worlds of Difference Inequality in the Aging Experience*. Thousand Oaks, CA: Pine forge Press.

The Boston Globe. 27 August 1991.

The Commonwealth Fund Commission Report. 1989. *Poverty and Poor Health Among Elderly Hispanic Americans*. Washington, D.C. The Commonwealth Fund Commission.

Trevino, Fernando M., M. Eugene Moyer, R. Burciaga Valdez, and Christine A. Stroup-Benham. 1991. "Health Insurance Coverage and Utilization of Health Services by Mexican Americans, Mainland Puerto Ricans, and Cuban Americans." *JAMA* (January 9th) 265 (2): 233-237.

Trevino, Margarita C. 1988. "A Comparative Analysis of Need, Access, and Utilization of Health and Human Services." In Steven R. Applewhite (Ed.), *The Hispanic Elderly in Transition*. Westport, CT: Greenwood Press: 61-71.

U. S. General Accounting Office. 1992. *Hispanic Access to Health Care: Significant Gaps Exist*. Washington, D.C.: Program Evaluation and Methodology Division (January) 1-26.

Velez, Josefina Estrada. 1979. "Use of Bilingual Materials in the Social Service System." *Hispanic Journal of Behavioral Sciences* 1 (4): 393-401.

Verbrugge, Lois M., James M. Lepkowski and Yuichi Imanaka. 1989. "Comorbidity and Its Impact on Disability." *The Milbank Quarterly* 67 (4): 450.

Wallace, Ruth A. and Alison Wolf. 1994. *Contemporary Sociological Theory: Continuing the Classical Tradition*. Englewood Cliffs, N.J.: Prentice -Hall, Inc.

Weeks, John R. and Jose B. Cuellar. 1981. "The Role of Family Members in the Helping Networks of Older People." *The Gerontologist* 21 (4): 388-394.

Williams, J. Sherwood, B. Krishna Singh, and L. D. Nelson. 1980. "Relative Size of Hispanic Populations and Hispanic/Anglo Poverty Ratios." *Hispanic Journal of Behavioral Sciences* 2 (3): 287-296.

Woerner, Louise. 1979. "The Hispanic Elderly: Meeting the Needs of a Special Population." *Civil Rights Digest* (spring) 3-11.

Zambrana, Ruth E., Rolando Merino, and Sarah Santana. 1979. "Health Services and the Puerto Rican Elderly." In Donald E. Gelfand and Alfred J. Kutzik (Eds.), *Ethnicity and Aging: Theory, Research and Policy.* New York: Springer Publishing Company: 308-319.

Zsembik, Barbara A. 1994. "Ethnic and Sociodemographic Correlates of the Use of Proxy Respondents: The National Survey of Hispanic Elderly People, 1988." *Research on Aging* 16 (4): 401-415.

Author Index

Subject Index